business-to-business bible

Titles in the *Work the Web* series

E-commerce, Simon Collin   0–471–49898–X
E-marketing, Simon Collin   0–471–49897–1
Business-to-Business Bible, Simon Collin   0–471–49896–3

WORK THE WEB

business-to-business bible

SIMON COLLIN

JOHN WILEY & SONS, LTD

Chichester · New York · Weinheim · Brisbane · Singapore · Toronto

Published in 2000 by John Wiley & Sons Ltd,
Baffins Lane, Chichester,
West Sussex PO19 1UD, England

National   01243 779777
International   (+44) 1243 779777
e-mail (for orders and customer service enquiries):
cs-books@wiley.co.uk
Visit our Home Page on http://www.wiley.co.uk
or http://www.wiley.com

Other Wiley Editorial Offices

John Wiley & Sons, Inc., 605 Third Avenue,
New York, NY 10158-0012, USA

WILEY-VCH Verlag GmbH, Pappelallee 3,
D-69469 Weinheim, Germany

Jacaranda Wiley Ltd, 33 Park Road, Milton,
Queensland 4064, Australia

John Wiley & Sons (Asia) Pte Ltd, 2 Clementi Loop #02-01,
Jin Xing Distripark, Singapore 129809

John Wiley & Sons (Canada) Ltd, 22 Worcester Road,
Rexdale, Ontario M9W 1L1, Canada

British Library Cataloguing in Publication Data

A catalogue record for this book is available from the British Library

ISBN 0-471-49896-3

Typeset in 10/12pt Palatino by Dorwyn Ltd, Rowlands Castle, Hants.

This book is printed on acid-free paper responsibly manufactured from sustainable
forestation, for which at least two trees are planted for each one used for paper
production.

contents

one   business resources on the Internet   1
business portals   2
business bodies   3

two   finding a business online   5
international directories   6
local UK business directories   7
general-purpose search engines   10
metasearchers   12

three   accounting   13
official sites   14
accountants   15
international accountants   16
accounting software   17

four   business advice   19
business advice   20
management gurus   21
management consultants   22
legal advice   22
patents and trademarks   23

five   business education   25
business schools – guides   25
business schools   26
language training   28

six   starting a business   29
starting a business   30
writing a business plan   31

	buying or selling a business	32
	franchises	33
	SOHO	33
seven ▧	**business to business**	35
	general	36
	getting the best price	37
	aerospace	38
	agriculture	39
	automotive industry	40
	barter	41
	cars and vans	42
	construction	43
	chemicals	44
	communications	44
	energy	45
	environment/utilities	46
	fashion	46
	food and drink	47
	hospitality	48
	healthcare	48
	high tech	49
	industry	50
	materials	51
	public sector	51
	science	51
	services	51
	surplus goods	51
eight ▧	**office supplies**	53
	equipment and furniture	54
	stationery	55
	postage	56
	courier companies	56
	telephones	57
	telephone over the Internet	58
	computer equipment	59
	computer supplies	60

	shareware libraries	60
	computer support	61
nine ▓	**offices and property**	63
	commercial property	64
	serviced offices	65
ten ▓	**financial management**	67
	business banking	68
	invoice factoring	69
	bankruptcy advice	70
	bankruptcy specialists	71
	business loans and finance	72
	grants	73
	financial advisors	74
	pensions and employee retirement guides	74
	pension companies	75
	credit cards	76
	insurance: office, liability and general	77
	motor insurance	78
	medical insurance	78
eleven ▓	**global business**	79
	translations	80
	general guides for export	80
	world economics	81
	business in Europe	83
	business in North America	86
	business in Central and South America	87
	business in India and subcontinent	88
	business in the Far East	88
	business in Australasia	89
	business in the Middle East	90
	business in Africa	90
twelve ▓	**human resources and staff**	91
	general HR sites	92
	workplace safety	93
	staff benefits	93
	testing and interviews	93

	finding staff	94
	workplace illness – stress management	95
	trades unions and professional bodies	96
thirteen	**news**	99
	news digests	99
	finding news websites	101
	general news	101
	business news	101
	country-specific news	102
	business magazines	103
fourteen	**reference and research**	105
	general reference	106
	dictionaries and encyclopaedias	106
	questions answered	107
	local information	107
	yellow pages	107
	government information	108
	company research	109
fifteen	**sales and marketing**	111
	general E-marketing information	112
	direct mail and e-mail	113
	renting e-mail lists	114
	exhibitions and conventions	114
	conference centres	115
	promotional materials	116
	contact management	118
	advertising agencies	118
	e-mail marketing	118
	banner advertising	119
	online advertising agencies	120
	press release services	120
sixteen	**building websites**	121
	advice for site builders	122
	webpage editors	122
	domain name registration	122
	Web databases	123

	website technical resources	124
	multimedia servers	124
	promoting websites	124
	what's new and award sites	125
	measuring response and Web analysis	126
seventeen ▨	**E-commerce**	127
	shopping carts	127
	turnkey shopping sites	128
	payment processing	130
	paying online	131
	consumer watchdogs	133
	secure websites	134
	digital signatures	135
	encryption	136
eighteen ▨	**stocks and shares**	137
	share portals	137
	market data and prices	138
	realtime share prices	140
	stock exchanges	141
	specialist investments	141
	futures and options	142
	online brokers	142
	new issues/IPOs	143
nineteen ▨	**travel**	145
	business travel guides	145
	guides and maps	146
	airlines	147
	airports	149
	travel agents	150
	personal jets	151
	hotels	151
	frequent flier schemes	152
twenty ▨	**discussing business**	153
	finding mailing lists	154
	discussion groups and chat forums	154
	E-zines	156

	finding newsgroups	156
	business newsgroups	157
	free e-mail accounts	158
appendix	**getting online**	161
	choosing an ISP	161
	getting on the Internet	162
	office net policy	164
	setting up the software	165
	electronic mail	167
	security and viruses	170
getting online –	e-mail software	173
directory	free e-mail accounts	173
	finding an e-mail address	173
	newsgroup readers	174
	finding and searching newsgroups	174
	management and filter software	174
	anti-virus software	174
glossary		175

business resources on the Internet

The Internet is one of the most effective resources that your company can use to improve efficiency in almost every department. It can help you research a new market, test a product, sell efficiently, streamline purchasing, promote your brand, find and manage staff, get the best deal on travel, find and equip and maintain your office.

This directory has been compiled to provide a quick and convenient resource to help you find websites. The directory has been organised into sections that cover almost every aspect of business on the Internet – from business advice to venture capital, finding staff to buying office supplies.

The directory is packed with more than 1700 websites that have been checked before adding them to this book – however, the Internet keeps changing and expanding and you might find that some of the website names have changed as companies are bought, sold or merged.

The book is divided into logical chapters, with sections for each type of website; if you want to know how to book a hotel room in Chicago, look to Chapter 19 and in the 'hotels' section. Similarly, if you want to trade with other businesses, look in Chapter 7 and choose the section that interests you – from 'chemicals' to 'fashion'.

The business area of the Net is, in general, seeing fantastic growth and change as companies rush to get on the Web. The first boom of the Net provided a mass of sites servicing consumers (for example, selling books, videos and clothes) – called business-to-consumer

(B2C), these sites are now more established, but seen as simply paving the way for the far bigger potential market-place of business-to-business (B2B).

Business-to-business sites try and provide a fast, efficient channel to help you get information, buy products or deal with businesses. For example, you can now find staff, stationery or new parts for your corporate jet with just a few clicks on specialist B2B sites. Some sites let you shop and buy consumables (such as office furniture, phones or stationery); other sites provide specialist auction forums where you can offer or bid for surplus or second-hand business goods – from a bulk load of paperclips to metal-working machinery.

If you are still planning a new start-up or if you are hoping to bring your business up to date and gain the latest advantage offered by the Internet, you are sure to find this book a useful starting point. And if you are new to the Internet, flip to the appendix on page 161 for a concise guide to getting your computer or your office network online and using all the resources on offer.

business portals

In the rest of this directory, lists of the specialist websites have been compiled that cover a particular subject, product or service. If you want to buy chemicals or agricultural machinery, office furniture or headed notepaper, there is a specialist website for each of these products. However, the Web is far more interesting than being just a simple shopping catalogue; one of the best places to start browsing is one of the big business portals.

These portal sites are superstores, advice centres and business directories rolled into one. They gather together material, services and advice from other sites and provide a central point of reference. If you want something in particular, use the rest of this directory to help find it quickly and efficiently. But if you have time to browse the Web, you will find these portals make a great starting point for your surfing.

AllBusiness.com   www.allbusiness.com
bCentral   www.bcentral.com

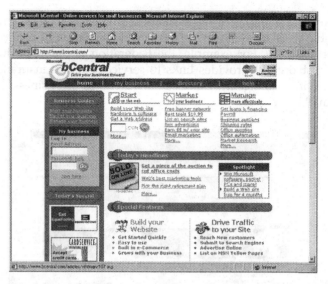

Figure 1.1 Microsoft's bCentral portal provides a central point for business news and services

Bloomberg	www.bloomberg.com
Dow Jones Business Directory	www.businessdirectory.dowjones.com
EOCenter	www.eocenter.com
FinanceWise	www.financewise.com
Inc. Online	www.inc.com
Killerbiz	www.killerbiz.com
Office.com	www.office.com
The Raging Bull	www.ragingbull.com
SmartAge	www.smartage.com
SmartOnline	www.smartonline.com

business bodies

British business has a whole range of business organisations working for their cause. Most aim their efforts on behalf of a particular group of businesses – for example, small businesses, business directors or manufacturing industries. However, they all provide valuable websites that are packed with information of use to their target audience. For example, the Federation of Small Businesses (www.fsb.org.uk) provides links to services such as insurance, financial and management advice, and archives of business guides for small businesses.

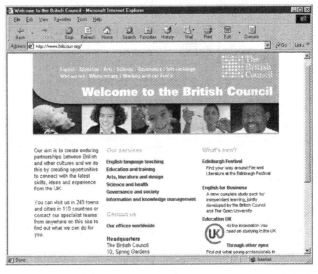

Figure 1.2 The British Council promotes and supports British exports, its culture and language

British Chambers of Commerce	www.britishchambers.org.uk
British Council	www.britcoun.org
British Safety Council	www.britishsafetycouncil.co.uk
British Standards Institute	www.bsi.org.uk
Confederation of British Industry (CBI)	www.cbi.org.uk
Federation of Small Businesses	www.fsb.org.uk
Institute of Directors	www.iod.co.uk
Health and Safety Executive	www.hse.gov.uk

finding a business online

One of the most frustrating aspects of the Internet is its sheer scale – there are millions of businesses online with interesting websites that could provide the perfect match for your company. The problem is in trying to find this particular website from the hundreds of millions of other hobbyist, enthusiast and crackpot sites that form the Web.

There are hundreds of general-purpose search engines on the Web (see page 10), such as Yahoo! and Excite! that will display thousands of matches to a simple query for a valve manufacturer or a specialist wholesaler. But you have no time to wade through these results to find which really is a useful business website, so instead, use one of the specialist business directories. These generally work rather like a Yellow Pages telephone directory, organising companies by section. You will find these guides great for:

■ finding new suppliers and potential distributors
■ finding the website of a particular company
■ finding a local specialist company
■ finding a company that offers products or services online

international directories

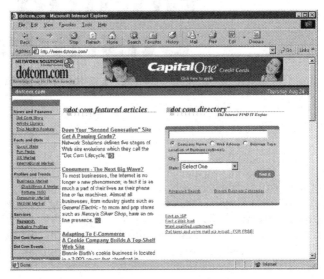

Figure 2.1   DotcomDirectory lets you find the website address of any company, or the owner of any website

555-1212.com Directory	www.555-1212.com
A Source	www.asource.com
AB Directory	www.comfind.com
BizExpose.com	www.bizexposure.com
BizWeb	www.bizweb.com
Business Seek	www.businesseek.com
CommerceInc	http://search.commerceinc.com
CompaniesOnline	www.companiesonline.com
Dot Com Directory	www.dotcomdirectory.com
Dow Jones Business Directory	www.businessdirectory.dowjones.com
EcoMall Companies	www.ecomall.com/biz/
ExpertFind	www.expertfind.com
Export Hotline Online	www.exporthotline.com

FirstList Mergers and Acquisitions	www.firstlist.com
GovWorks	www.govworks.com
Grail Search	www.grailsearch.com
Greatinfo.Com	www.greatinfo.com
Hoover's Online	www.hoovers.com
IndustryLink	www.industrylink.com
Information Please	www.infoplease.looksmart.com
IntelliSearch	www.intellisearchnow.com
Minority Business Directory	www.mbnet.com
NYSE – Listed Companies	www.nyse.com
onVia	www.onvia.com
Pronet Canadian Companies	www.pronet.ca
Rescue Island – Business Search	www.rescueisland.com
Standard & Poor's 500	www.spglobal.com/500mainframe.html
Starting Point Business Categories	www.stpt.com
Startup Zone	www.startupzone.com
The Biz	www.thebiz.co.uk
Thomas Regional Directories	www.thomasregional.com
TopStartups.com	www.topstartups.com
VerticalNet	www.verticalnet.com
ZDNet Company Finder New!	www.zdnet.com/companyfinder/

local UK business directories

@skypages	www.skypages.com/uk
Ask Alex	www.askalex.co.uk
Berkshire Local Pages	www.berkshire.cc

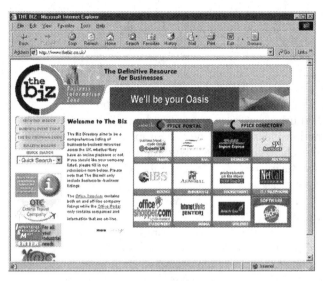

Figure 2.2 TheBiz provides a comprehensive directory of Web-based companies

Black Country Internet Directory	www.blackcountry.co.uk
Bradford Business Directory	www.bradford.gov.uk/business/business-directory
Bristol Directory	http://bristol.netgates.co.uk
Business Centre	www.web-centre.co.uk/business.htm
CambSearch	www.cambsearch.co.uk
CAMBWeb	www.cambweb.co.uk/cambweb/business
Channel Islands Internet Directory	http://jsem.simplenet.com/ci
Citypages	www.citypages.co.uk
Companies Database	www.ukbusinessnet.com
Companies House	www.companies-house.gov.uk
Dorset Business Index	www.dorsetweb.co.uk/business
Dorset List, The	www.artisan-inter.net/dorsetlist
East Grinstead Area Businesses	www.egnet.co.uk
East Midlands Net	www.eastmidlands.net

Enterprise Zone	www.enterprisezone.org.uk
Essex Web	www.essexweb.co.uk
Europages	www.europages.com
FifeInfo	www.fifeinfo.co.uk
Freepages	www.freepages.co.uk
Glazgow – Business	www.glazgow.com/business
Hackney Business Directory	www.poptel.org.uk/hackney-business
Henley-on-Thames Classified Business Directory	www.henley-on-thames.com
Huddersfield Online Directory	www.huddnet.co.uk
INbusiness	www.inbusiness.co.uk
Infolinks	www.infolinks.net
Internet Pages	www.the-internet-pages.co.uk
Kelly's	www.kellys.reedinfo.co.uk
Kent-Business.Net	www.kent-business.net
Lincolnshire Business & Community Directory	www.lincolnshire.net
London Business Directory	www.absite.com/london
Mailhouse – Ireland	www.mailhouse-ireland.com
Manxdirectory	www.manxdirectory.com
North of England Online	www.neon.org.uk
Northamptonshire Business Pages	www.northamptonshire.co.uk
Scoot	www.scoot.co.uk
Scotland.org	www.scotland.org
Somerset Business Directory	www.exclaim.demon.co.uk/somerset
States of Jersey – Business	www.jersey.gov.uk
The Biz	www.thebiz.co.uk
UK Business Directory	www.milfac.co.uk/bisindex.html

UK Directory	www.ukdirectory.co.uk
UK Yellow Web	www.yell.co.uk
Company A-Z	
Yell	www.yell.co.uk

general-purpose search engines

To find information rather than a particular company's website, you will need to turn to a general-purpose search engine. These websites contain a vast index of websites that you can search. Type in your search word or query expression and you will get a list of websites that match this term. The problem with general-purpose search engines is the quantity of, often poor quality, results. Search for *export advice* and you will get over one million matching websites – with no guide to help you find the best or the most sensible.

Add to this the fact that the number of new websites is growing so fast that none of these search engines can claim to cover the whole Web – in fact, they generally cover fewer than half the websites in existence – and you have a less than perfect solution. To get around these problems, there are three solutions:

1. Try and index every website on the Web: the biggest search engines such as AltaVista, Excite, Lycos, and Northern Light all spend a lot of their time hunting out new sites to add to their indices.
2. Be selective – directories such as Yahoo!, Scoot and Yell have definite criteria for adding websites and so limit themselves to tens or hundreds of thousands of sites (compared to the tens of millions of the big search engines).
3. You can review all the sites – this is by far the most time-consuming process because it requires human editors to visit the sites and write a summary. But it is the most useful for surfers who want an impartial view. This policy is used to good effect by About and LookSmart to provide a limited, but impartial guide to the sites on offer.

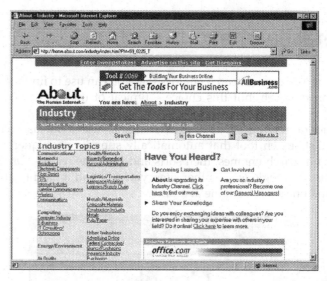

Figure 2.3 About provides a directory, search engine and informed expert advice on almost every popular subject

About	www.about.com
AltaVista	www.altavista.com
Euroseek	www.euroseek.net
Excite!	www.excite.co.uk
G.O.D.	www.god.co.uk
HotBot	www.hotbot.com
Infoseek	www.infoseek.com
LookSmart	www.looksmart.co.uk
Lycos	www.lycos.co.uk
Magellan	http://magellan.excite.com
Northern Light	www.northernlight.com
Scoot	www.scoot.co.uk
UKPlus	www.ukplus.com
WebCrawler	www.webcrawler.com
Yahoo!	www.yahoo.com
Yell	www.yell.co.uk

metasearchers

There are dozens of search engines that you can use to find information on the Web, but this choice – typical of the Net – creates as many problems as it solves. Which search engine should you use? Instead of relying on one search engine, use a metasearcher – specialist search tool that automatically submits your query to all the main search engines, then sorts and rates the results. Once you start using Google or the other sites, you will find it hard to go back to using one search engine at a time.

Figure 2.4   Google looks simple, but it provides one of the neatest ways of quizzing dozens of search engines at once

AllOneSearch	www.allonesearch.com
AskJeeves	www.askjeeves.com
DogPile	www.dogpile.com
Google!	www.google.com
InferenceFind	www.infind.com
MetaCrawler	www.metacrawler.com
Savvy Search	www.savvysearch.com

accounting

The Web provides a great resource centre for anyone dealing with their accounts. If you are a small business struggling with your quarterly or year-end accounts, there are sites that provide advice or software to make the job easier. Or, best of all, use one of the online directories to find a professional accountant to manage your books for you. And if you are an accounting professional, you can keep up to date with the latest news and regulations from your official body's websites.

For companies willing to embrace the Internet whole-heartedly, there are several ways it can help you manage your accounts. Perhaps the most exciting is the integration of online business bank accounts and accounting software. Almost every high-street bank now offers its business customers Internet access to their account details. This lets you shuffle money from one account to another, pay bills and check the statements (see page 68 for more details). Accounting software from companies such as Intuit and Sage will interrogate your online business account and download all the information to your computer. You can now analyse and manipulate the information to provide your monthly accounts and so help manage your cash flow.

The final part of the puzzle has just been provided by the UK government, which now allows businesses (and individuals) to file their tax forms over the Net – and for a limited period, you will get a £50 credit for doing this. Other countries, including the US and Australia, have had this system in place for years, and US-specific accounting software from Intuit and others provides a menu option to directly file your accounts data to the US Inland Revenue.

official sites

The UK and US revenue services both provide useful, informative (and occasionally witty) websites. They are packed with all the official directives and legal texts, together with simple guides to help new businesses manage the subject. If you are looking for an official site in any other country, use the excellent Taxsites (www. taxsites.com) directory of worldwide websites or, for UK-specific information, try the comprehensive UK Taxation Directory (www.uktax.demon.co.uk).

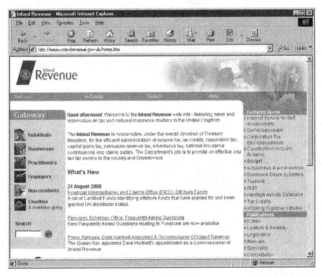

Figure 3.1 Advice and official forms – with guidance when filling them in – for business and personal users at the Inland Revenue

The Inland Revenue, UK   www.inlandrevenue.gov.uk
Internal Revenue Service   www.irs.ustreas.gov/prod/bus_info/
  USA

accountants

To help you manage your accounts, provide year-end auditing or day-to-day bookkeeping, you should contact a qualified accountant – and preferably, one who is a specialist in your industry. To help you find a qualified professional, use one of these online directories; in the UK, an accountant should be a member of a professional accounting body such as the ACCA (www.acca.co.uk). Visit the directory sites, type in your location and requirements and you will see a list of local experts who can help you manage every aspect of your finances, from cash flow to tax, payroll to VAT.

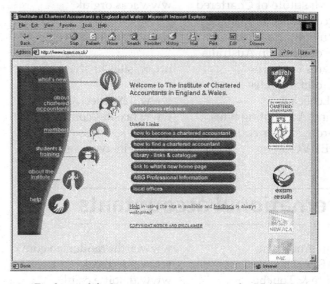

Figure 3.2   Find a qualified accountant near you at the ICAEW institute site

ABIAF (Association of British   www.abiaf.co.uk
  Independent Accounting
  Firms)
ACCA (Association of   www.acca.co.uk
  Chartered Certified
  Accountants)

Accountant finder	www.cpafinder.com
AccountantsDotCom	www.accountantsdotcom.com
Accountant-Search.com	www.accountant-search.com
Chartered Accountants Directory	www.chartered-accountants.co.uk
Chartered Institute of Taxation	www.tax.org.uk
CPA Firms	www.cpafirms.com
CPA Online	www.cpaonline.com.au
CyberAccountant	www.cyber-cpa.com
EuroAsPa	www.euroaspa.com
ICAEW (Institute of Chartered Accountants of England and Wales)	www.icaew.co.uk
ICAS (Institute of Chartered Accountants of Scotland)	www.icas.org.uk
Institute of Chartered Accountants in Australia	www.icaa.org.au
Krislyn's Favourite Accounting Sites	http://sites.krislyn.com/acct.htm
PAYEcheck	www.payecheck.co.uk
Tax and Accounting Sites	www.taxsites.com
Taxprofessionals.com	www.taxprofessionals.com
TriNET VCO	www.trinetvco.com

international accountants

Arthur Andersen	www.arthurandersen.com
BDO Stoy Hayward	www.bdo.co.uk
Deloitte & Touche	www.deloitte.co.uk
Ernst & Young	www.ernsty.co.uk
Kidsons Impey	www.kidsons.co.uk
KPMG	www.kpmg.com
PriceWaterhouseCoopers	www.pwcglobal.com

accounting software

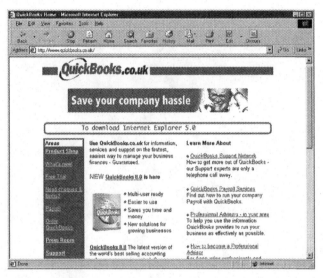

Figure 3.3 Intuit's QuickBooks is one way for small businesses to computerize their accounts

Accounting Software Systems	www.2020software.com
Accubooks 2000	www.accubooks2000.com
AccPac	www.accpac.com
DacEasy	www.daceasy.com
Great Plains	www.gps.com
Money	www.microsoft.com/money/
MYOB	www.myob.com
Peachtree Accounting	www.peachtree.com
QuickBooks	www.quickbooks.com
QuickTax	www.quicktax.co.uk
ResourcePhoenix	www.resourcephoenix.com
Sage	www.sage.co.uk
TaxCalc	www.idp.co.uk
TaxSaver	www.microsoft.com

business
advice

Every business person needs advice on some aspect of their company: if you are the owner, you might be a technical expert, but perhaps do not know every line on employment rights; if you are a manager, you might want advice on forecasting or cash flow. Whatever your requirement, you will find the Internet is packed with sites offering advice, guides and information on just about every part of business – from marketing to accounts, sales to manufacturing.

Almost all the advice and information you will find online is free – and you can even read the latest thoughts and theories from some of the best-known gurus (most of whom are canny enough to have their own commercial websites). And if you do not have time to do the research, read up and implement the advice from the Internet, you can always use it to find a professional consultant who will be able to do all this for you.

Much of the content online is aimed at entrepreneurs and those starting out in business; there are guides from official bodies, such as Business Link, or magazines, such as Inc. and Fast Company. However, there is still masses of information for anyone looking for more specialist or advanced guides from organisations such as the American Management Association and WilsonWeb. And if you want to expand your knowledge or train in a new area, look to pages 25–28 for business schools online.

business advice

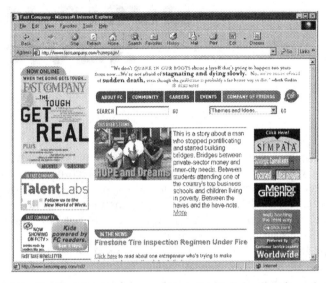

Figure 4.1 The Fast Company magazine is the style leader of new business methods

AllBusiness.com	www.allbusiness.com
American Express Small Business Exchange	www.americanexpress.com/smallbusiness/
American Management Association	www.amanet.org
Business Associations	www.ibf.com/ba/ibba.htm
Business Link	www.businesslink.co.uk
Business Resource Center	www.morebusiness.com
CommerceNet	www.commerce.net
Enterprise Zone	www.enterprisezone.org.uk
EnterWeb	www.enterweb.org
Entrepreneurial Edge Online	www.edgeonline.com
EntreWorld	www.entreworld.org
Fast Company	www.fastcompany.com
Garage.com	www.garage.com
GovWorks	www.govworks.com

Guru	www.guru.com
Inc. Online	www.inc.com
Microsoft bCentral	www.bcentral.com
Office.com	www.office.com
Online Women's Business Center	www.onlinewbc.org
SmartOnline	www.smartonline.com
WilsonWeb	www.wilsonweb.com

management gurus

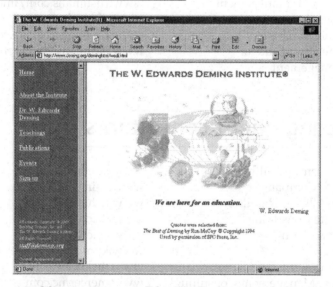

Figure 4.2 Management guru Edwards Deming moves his ideas and theories onto the Web

Alliance of Consultants	www.allianceofconsultants.com
American Management Association	www.amanet.org
Edwards Deming: his teachings	www.deming.org
Demings 14 Points	http://deming.ces.clemson.edu
Peter F. Drucker	www.drucker.org

Electronic Intelligence management library	www.anbar.co.uk/ management
The Glass Ceiling	www.theglassceiling.com
Charles Handy: The Search for Meaning	www.drucker.org/ leaderbooks/L2L/ summer97/handy.html
Harvard Business School Publishing	www.hbsp.harvard.edu
Leadership Communications for the 21st Century	www.lc21.com
Management General	www.mgeneral.com
Selection of Management Consultants	www.rushmans.com/imc/ page6.html
TrainingSuperSite	www.trainingsupersite.com
Women's Institute of Management	www.jaring.my/wimnet

management consultants

Andersen Consulting	www.ac.com
Bain & Company	www.bain.com
Booz-Allen & Hamilton	www.bah.com
Deloitte Consulting	www.dc.com
Ernst & Young	www.ey.com
KPMG	www.kpmg.com
McKinsey & Co.	www.mckinsey.com
Mercer Management Consulting	www.mercermc.com

legal advice

If you want an expert to check over or draw up a contract, or if you are having a dispute with another company, you will need a good lawyer. For contracts you should look to a lawyer specialising in your particular industry – search one of these online databases or visit the official Law Society site for links to other specialist directories. And if you want to hire a lawyer in another country, try one of the international directories or contact the local British Council office (www. britcoun.org) which might be able to help recommend a company.

ABA Network Lawyer Locator	www.abanet.org/martindale.html
Attorney Net	www.attorneynet.com
CaseMatch	www.casematch.com
CataLaw Legal Directories	www.catalaw.com
Law Central	www.lawcentral.co.uk
Law Society	www.lawsoc.org.uk
UK Employment Law	www.emplaw.co.uk
UK Legal	www.uklegal.com
World Law Guide	www.lexadin.nl/wlg/

patents and trademarks

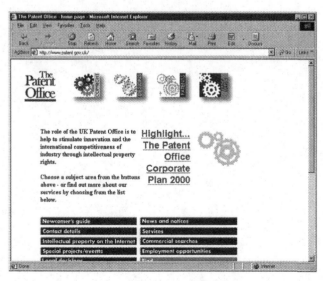

Figure 4.3 Invented a new gizmo? Patent advice from the government's official site

All about Trademarks	www.ggmark.com
American Intellectual Property Law Association	www.aipla.org
Corporate Intelligence	www.1790.com
European Patent Office	www.epo.co.at/epo/
IBM Patent Server	www.patents.ibm.com
Institute of Trademark Attorneys	www.itma.org.uk
INTA	www.inta.org
KuesterLaw	www.kuesterlaw.com
Trademark Database	www.uspto.gov/tmdb/index.html
Patent Cafe	www.patentcafe.com
The Patent Office	www.patent.gov.uk
US Patents	www.uspto.gov

business education

Business courses can help you tackle a specialist subject, for example marketing or management, or study for an MBA to help you understand how best to plan and view the 'big picture' for a company's development and growth. And, of course, a qualification always helps when you want to move job.

The Internet has guides to business schools and colleges around the world – select the subject and location and you will see a list of schools that offer full or part-time courses. Once you have found a course that is of interest, visit the school's website (almost every educational establishment, not just business schools, has a website) to find out more. Some schools specialise in distance learning – traditionally this was by post or telephone; now it is Web-based lessons and e-mail feedback from your tutors.

business schools – guides

Association of Business Schools www.the-abs.org.uk
Bschool.com www.bschool.com
Business Education on the Internet http://bizednet.bris.ac.uk
EBEA www.bized.ac.uk/ebea
Kaplan's Business School 'Zine www.kaplan.com/gmat/
MBA Explorer www.gmat.org
MBA Plaza www.mbaplaza.com

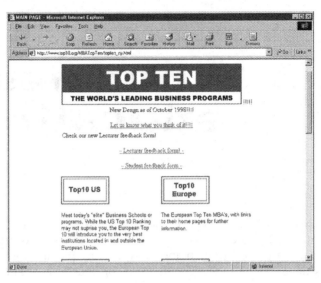

Figure 5.1 To find out which is best, check the top ten schools

Official MBA Guide – Unicorn Research	http://mba.us.com/guide/
The MBA Tour	www.thembatour.com
Top 10	www.top10.org

business schools

Asian Institute of Management	www.aim.edu.ph
Aston Business School	www.abs.aston.ac.uk
Athens University of Economics and Business	www.aueb.gr/gb/
Australian Graduate School of Management	www.agsm.unsw.edu.au
Ceram ESC Nice Sophia Antipolis	www.ceram.edu
China Europe International Business School (CEIBS)	www.ceibs.edu
Chinese University of Hong Kong Faculty of Business Administration	www.cuhk.edu.hk/baf/

Figure 5.2 The famous business school provides reports, materials – and contacts if you want to apply

College of Estate Management	www.cem.ac.uk
Concordia University Faculty of Commerce and Administration	www.concordia.ca
Copenhagen Business School	www.cbs.dk
Cranfield School of Management	www.cranfield.ac.uk/som
Czech Management Center Graduate School of Business	www.cmc.cz
Dalhousie University Faculty of Management	www.mgmt.dal.ca
Durham University Business School	www.dur.ac.uk
Harvard University – Harvard Business School	www.hbs.edu
Henley Management College	www.henleymc.ac.uk
Heriot-Watt University Edinburgh Business School	www.ebs.hw.ac.uk
Imperial College Management School	http://graph.ms.ic.ac.uk
INSEAD	www.insead.fr
International Institute for Management Development (IMD)	www.imd.ch

International Management Institute — www.timi.edu
Irish Management Institute — www.imi.ie
King's College Management Centre — www.kcl.ac.uk
Kobe University School of Business — www.kobe_u.ac.jp
London Business School — www.lbs.lon.ac.uk
London School of Economics — www.blpes.lse.ac.uk
Manchester Business School — www.mbs.ac.uk
MIT — www.mit.edu
Oxford University Said Business School — www.sbs.ox.ac.uk
Princeton — www.princeton.edu
Rutgers School of Business – Camden — www.rutgers.edu
Sheffield Hallam University — www.mbainfo.org
University of Dublin Trinity College School of Business Studies — www.tcd.ie
University of Manchester – Manchester Business School — www.mbs.ac.uk
University of Melbourne Faculty of Economics and Commerce — www.ecom.unimelb.edu.au
University of Navarra International Graduate School of Management (IESE) — www.iese.edu
Vienna University of Economics and Business Administration — www.wu_wien.ac.at
Yale University — www.yale.edu

language training

Association for Language Learning — www.languagelearn.co.uk
Centro Culturale Conero — www.linguaitaliana.com/inglese/courses.htm
Commercial Language Training — www.languagetraining.co.uk
Europa Pages — www.atlas.co.uk/efl
Institute of Linguists — www.iol.org.uk

starting a business

Starting a new business can be a daunting task. You might have a fantastic idea for a product or service, but few other jobs prepare you for the mechanics of starting and running a company. To successfully start and run a business you need your good idea, clear vision of how to deliver it to your customers and a polyglot personality that can cope with the minutiae of day-to-day jobs from accounting to marketing, VAT to corporate tax.

The Web is a great resource for anyone thinking of starting a business, or for someone who is running their own company. You will find expert guides and archives of advice and tips covering just about every task you are likely to encounter. Some sites specialise in one area, such as marketing or tax planning (see the relevant sections in this directory), but there are a range of large websites aimed at entrepreneurs. Some are government-sponsored, others have a commercial feel and offer goods and services (to pay for the expert advice), while many still use material from business magazines or specialist companies, such as accountants and lawyers. If you want advice on the step-by-step process on how to set up your company, or how to hire (or fire) your first employee, there is plenty of material on offer.

A popular way of starting a business is to set up a franchised operation of a successful, proven idea. Just about any good business idea has been spun off into a franchise; you pay an initial fee for a kit of materials, advice and support, and often a percentage of your turnover or profits back to the franchiser.

Most of the fast-food chains, sandwich shops, garages and newsagents are run in this way, providing an instant nationwide (sometimes international) brand awareness for a modest start up fee. Before you launch into this business world, make sure that you study the resources online – from case studies to business advice offering the ups and downs of a franchise operation. You will find the main franchise operators are members of a national organisation and this provides a degree of protection against poor quality and fraud.

starting a business

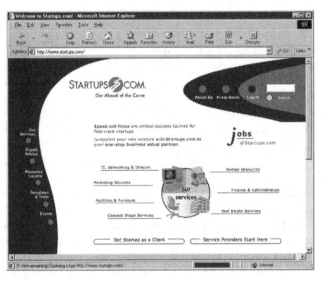

Figure 6.1   Startups.com provides Web-based help on launching your new business

BT Partnership	www.partnership.bt.com
Corporate	www.corporate.com
New Business Kit	www.new-business.co.uk
Small Business Administration	www.sba.gov
StartUps.com	www.startups.com
Your Business – Microsoft UK	www.microsoft.com/uk/yourbusiness/

writing a business plan

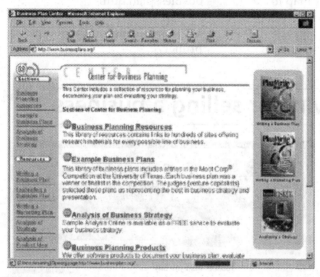

Figure 6.2 BusinessPlans offers help and tools to master the critical first step for any start-up, which is a solid business plan

BizPlanIt	www.bizplanit.com/vplan.htm
BizPlus Small Business Info	www.bizplus.com/zinfo/info.html
Bplans.com	www.bplans.com
Business Plan Outline	www.ntia.doc.gov/opadhome/mtdpweb/ busplano.htm
Business Resource Software	www.businessplans.org
BusinessTown.com	www.businesstown.com/planning/
CCH Business Owner's Toolkit	www.toolkit.cch.com
Edge Online Business Builders	http://edge.lowe.org/resource/bizbuild
Managing a Young Growing Business	www.triple-m.com/mmmcomm.htm
NEBS Business Tips	www.nebs.com/nmq.html

Plan Village	www.planvillage.com
PlanWare	www.planware.org
SBA Business Plan Roadmap to Success	www.sbaonline.sba.gov/starting/businessplan.html
Small Business Primer	www.morebusiness.com/getting_started/primer/

buying or selling a business

Figure 6.3 To buy a ready-made company, search a directory such as BuzBuySell

BizBuySell	www.bizbuysell.com
Business For You	www.business4u.com
Businesses for Sale	www.businessforsale.com
Daltons	www.daltons.co.uk
Exchange and Mart	www.exchangeandmart.co.uk
Franchise Solutions, Inc.	www.franchisesolutions.com
M&A Marketplace	www.mergernetwork.com

Moneytree   www.cargobay.com
Moore, Wood & Cockram www.mwclicproperty.demon.co.uk
Relocatable Business   www.relocatable.com

franchises

American Association of Franchisees & Dealers	www.aafd.org
The Australia Franchise Council	www.fca.com.au
Be the Boss	www.betheboss.com
The British Franchise Association	www.british-franchise.org.uk
Canadian Business Franchise Magazine	www.cgb.ca
Centercourt	www.centercourt.com
Federal Trade Commission – Franchises	www.ftc.gov/bcp/franchise/
FranchiseNet	www.franchise.net.au
The Franchise Registry	www.franchiseregistry.com
FranInfo	www.franinfo.co.uk
Franchising and franchises	www.franchisedirect.co.uk
Planet Smoothie	www.planetsmoothie.com
Subway	www.subway.com

SOHO (small office/home office)

Business Matters	www.business.knowledge.com
Home-based Business	www.smartbiz.com/sbs/cats/home.htm
Home Office Association of America	www.hoaa.com
Small Business 2000	www.sb2000.com
The Small Business Advisor	www.isquare.com

Smart Business Super Site	www.smartbiz.com
Yahoo! Small Business Information	uk.dir.yahoo.com/ Business_and_Economy/ Small_Business_Information/

business to business

The one area of the Web to have rocketed in popularity is the business to business (B2B) market, offering products and services between businesses. This sector of the Web is now projected to outclass the first phase of E-commerce (business to consumer or web-based retail) by providing an efficient, streamlined, but fantastically diverse, catalogue of products.

You can buy just about anything for your company cheaply and efficiently; some sites are simple Web versions of a mail-order office supplier, providing stationery, furniture and other office kit. Other sites embrace the potential of the Internet in a more creative fashion and let you – the customer – request bids from suppliers for a particular order. If you want to get quotes for the production of your next catalogue, put up a request on a central procurement site such as Mondus and wait for the bids to arrive.

Alternatively, use the online business auctions to get rid of your surplus products or to snap up a bargain of your own – these are particularly popular for agricultural machinery and second-hand computers and office furniture. Lastly, there is direct business to business in which customers find new suppliers and then route orders (and even payment) directly over the net, cutting out excessive paperwork and administration.

general

These vast sites provide a central point where you will find suppliers of just about everything your business needs – from printing to marketing, office supplies to travel arrangements. Some of these sites let you place an order online and ask for bids for the job; others are simple gateways to a wide range of online shops. Try one of these sites the next time you need supplies and see how the service (and price) compares with your traditional supplier.

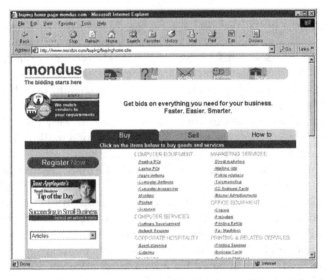

Figure 7.1 Publish your requirements and let suppliers bid for the job, with Mondus

b2bnow	www.b2bnow.com
b2bstores	www.b2bstores.com
B2BToday	www.B2BToday.com
BizBuyer	www.bizbuyer.com
Exchange & Mart	www.exchangeandmart.co.uk
Killerbiz	www.killerbiz.com
MarketSite	www.marketsite.net

Mondus   www.mondus.com
OrderZone   www.orderzone.com

getting the best price

The Net is full of online shops, but just as in a real shopping mall, you can be sure that one shop will have a special offer on paperclips while another has a sale of filing cabinets. To help you get the best from the online shops, use one of the comparison tools that will automatically quiz a range of shops and display the best prices (and availability) for your particular product. In the US, sites such as MySimon let you compare the prices of hundreds of different goods – from TVs to furniture – but in the UK, the equivalent sites such as ShopSmart are generally limited to simpler products such as books, videos and CDs.

As well as using the Web to get the best price for your supplies, you can use specialist sites such as Kura to compare the prices of

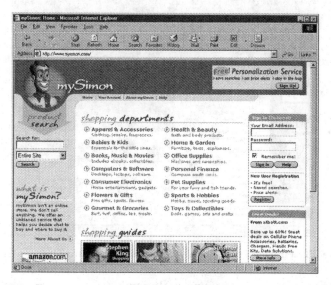

Figure 7.2 Ensure you get the best price; MySimon compares hundreds of online shops

utilities – telephone, gas, electricity or water – and let you see the deals on offer and show you what is cheapest for your needs.

Bottom Dollar	www.bottomdollar.com
BuyBuddy	www.buybuddy.com
buy.co.uk	www.buy.co.uk
Cheaper Calls UK	http://cheapercalls.8m.com
EvenBetter	www.evenbetter.com
Kura	www.kura.co.uk
MySimon	www.mysimon.com
Taxi	www.mytaxi.co.uk
ShopSmart	www.shopsmart.co.uk

aerospace

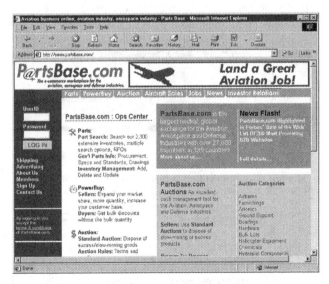

Figure 7.3 Find aero parts with specialist supplier PartsBase

| Avolo | www.avolo.com |
| ILSmart | www.ilsmart.com |

PartsBase.com	www.partsbase.com
Source One Spares	www.sourceonespares.com
TradeAir	www.tradeair.com

agriculture

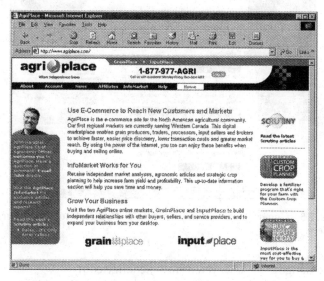

Figure 7.4 Information, advice and trade at AgriPlace

Agrilink Directory	www.agrilink.co.uk
AgriPlace	www.agriplace.com
CattleinfoNet	www.cattleinfonet.com
e-Greenbiz.com	www.e-greenbiz.com
Farmbid.com	www.farmbid.com
Farms.com	www.farms.com
FoodTrader.com	www.foodtrader.com
GrainPlace	www.grainplace.com
Rooster.com	www.rooster.com
Tradingproduce.com	www.tradingproduce.com

automotive industry

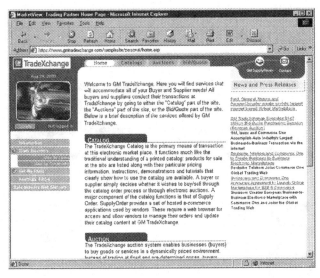

Figure 7.5 General Motors implements B2B direct to its dealers and suppliers

auto-xchange	www.auto-xchange.com
AutoTradeCenter	www.autotradecenter.com
bbcn.com	www.bbcn.com
CarParts.com	www.carparts.com
Covisint	www.covisint.com
GM TradeXchange	www.gmtradexchange.com
iStarXchange	www.istarxchange.com
The Cobalt Group	www.cobaltgroup.com
TradingCars.com	www.tradingcars.com
Wrenchead.com	www.wrenchead.com

barter

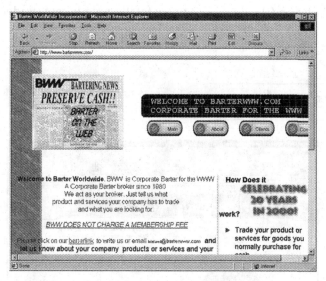

Figure 7.6 Swap your goods for something else using barter or specialist broker Barterwww.com

AAA Barter	www.aaabarter.com
Art of Barter	www.artofbarter.com
Barter Advantage	www.barteradv.com
Barter Brokers International	www.barterbrokers.com
Barter Business Exchange Incorporated	www.ncbarter.com
Barter Business Network	www.bbnetwork.com
Barter Connections Incorporated	www.barterconnection.com
Barter Online UK	www.barter-online.co.uk
Barter WorldWide	http://barterwww.com
Barter.com	www.barter.com
Bartercard International	www.bartercard.com

BarterTrust.com	www.bartertrust.com
BigVine.com	www.bigvine.com
Continental Trade Exchange	www.ctebarter.com
ICE Barter and Trade Exchange	www.totally-unique.com/tradepost
ICON International	www.icon-intl.com

cars and vans

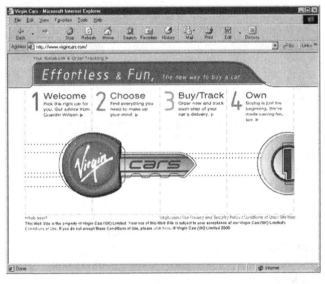

Figure 7.7 Source your new company cars at European prices with VirginCars

autobytel.com	www.autobytel.com
AutoExpress	www.autoexpress.co.uk
AutoTrader	www.autotrader.co.uk
British Vehicle and Leasing Association	www.bvrla.co.uk
Carsource	www.carsource.co.uk

Exchange & Mart	www.exchangeandmart.co.uk
New Car Net	www.new-car-net.co.uk
Vanfinder	www.vanfinder.co.uk
VirginCars	www.virgin-cars.co.uk
WhatCar?	www.whatcar.co.uk

construction

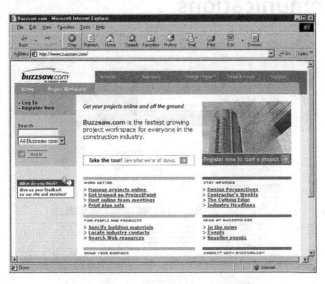

Figure 7.8 Buzzsaw provides a central trading point for the construction industry

Building Supplies	www.buildingsuppliersweb.com
Buzzsaw	www.buzzsaw.com
Grainger	www.grainger.com
bLiquid.com	www.bliquid.com
Bricsnet	www.bricsnet.com
BuildNET	www.buildnet.com
BuildPoint.com	www.buildpoint.com
Ironmax	www.ironmax.com
TradeYard Construction	http://construction.tradeyard.com

chemicals

CheMatch.com	www.chematch.com
ChemConnect	www.chemconnct.com
Chemdex	www.chemdex.com

communications

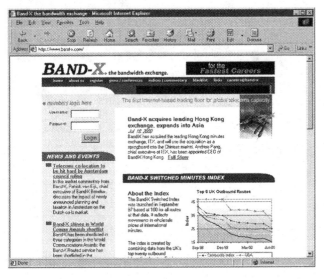

Figure 7.9 Band-X provides a specialist site where you can trade available bandwidth

ArbiNet – Exchange	www.arbinet.com
Band-X	www.band-x.com
Digital Broadcasting.com	www.digitalbroadcasting.com
Fiber Optics Online	www.fiberopticsonline.com
Photonics Online	www.photonicsonline.com
Premises Networks.com	www.premisesnetworks.com
RF Globalnet	www.rfglobalnet.com

Wireless Design Online	www.wirelessdesignonline.com
Wireless Networks Online	www.wirelessnetworksonline.com

energy

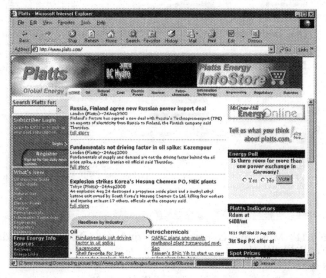

Figure 7.10　Keep up to date with the news source for the energy market, Platts

AltraNet	www.altra.net
Standard & Poors Platt's	www.platts.com
ElectricNet	www.electricnet.com
Hydrocarbon Online	www.hydrocarbononline.com
Oil and Gas Online	www.oilandgasonline.com
Power Online	www.poweronline.com

environment/utilities

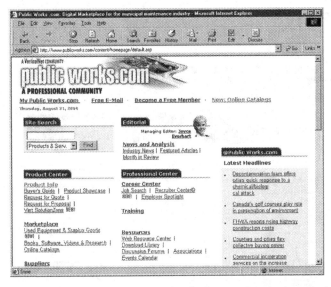

Figure 7.11 Municipal contractors can find out what is new and trade online at PublicWorks

Pollution Online	www.pollutiononline.com
Public Works.com	www.publicworks.com
Safety Online	www.safetyonline.com
Solid Waste.com	www.solidwaste.com
Water Online	www.wateronline.com

fashion

fashionbyauction.com	www.fashionbyauction.com
LeatherXchange.com	www.leatherxchange.com

food and drink

Figure 7.12 FoodTrader provides a central point to trade food products

Agribuys.com	www.agribuys.com
BevAccess.com	www.BevAccess.com
buyproduce.com	www.buyproduce.com
Direct 2 Government	www.Direct2Government.com
ecFood.com	www.ecfood.com
eFruit International	www.efruitinternational.com
eGrocery.com	www.egrocery.com
enuts.com	www.enuts.com
eSkye.com	www.eskye.com
Foodhunter	www.foodhunter.net
FoodTrader.com	www.foodtrader.com
Global Food Exchange.com	www.globalfoodexchange.com
Gofish.com	www.gofish.com
Professional Brewer	www.professionalbrewer.com
SellMEAT	www.sellmeat.com
Tradingproduce.com	www.tradingproduce.com

WineryExchange	www.wineryexchange.com
Bakery Online	www.bakeryonline.com
Beverage Online	www.beverageonline.com
Dairy Network.com	www.dairynetwork.com
Food Ingredients Online	www.foodingredientsonline.com
Food Online	www.foodonline.com
Meat and Poultry Online	www.meatandpoultryonline.com
Packaging Network.com	www.packagingnetwork.com

hospitality

E-Hospitality.com	www.e-hospitality.com
Foodservice Central.com	www.foodservicecentral.com
Grocery Central.com	www.grocerycentral.com

healthcare

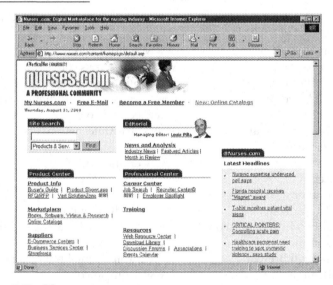

Figure 7.13   Nurses.com

E-Dental.com	www.e-dental.com
Home Health Provider.com	www.homehealthprovider.com
Hospital Network.com	www.hospitalnetwork.com
Long Term Care Provider.com	www.longtermcareprovider.com
Nurses.com	www.nurses.com

high tech

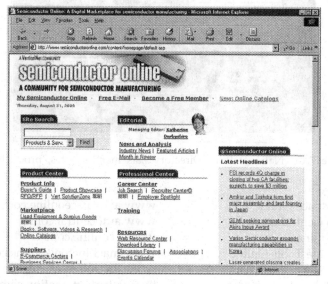

Figure 7.14 Semiconductor online

ElectronicsWeb	www.electronicsweb.com
Embedded Technology.com	www.embeddedtechnology.com
Medical Design Online	www.medicaldesignonline.com
Semiconductor Online	www.semiconductoronline.com
Test and Measurement.com	www.testandmeasurement.com

industry

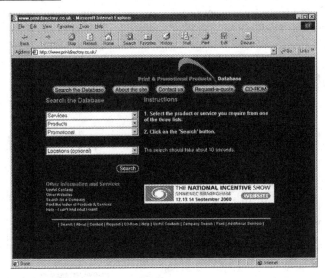

Figure 7.15 National Print Directory lists member sites, products and services

Aerospace Online	www.aerospaceonline.com
Auto Central.com	www.autocentral.com
EC Online	www.econline.com
Machine Tools Online	www.machinetoolsonline.com
Metrology World.com	www.metrologyworld.com
Plant Automation.com	www.plantautomation.com
Surface Finishing.com	www.surfacefinishing.com
Tooling Online	www.toolingonline.com
Adhesives and Sealants.com	www.adhesivesandsealants.com
Chemical Online	www.chemicalonline.com
Pharmaceutical Online	www.pharmaceuticalonline.com
Pulp & Paper Online	www.pulpandpaperonline.com
TextileWeb	www.textileweb.com
Applegate Electronics Directory	www.apgate.com/elec
Elevation's Elevation Emporium	www.elevation.co.uk
National Print Directory	www.printdirectory.co.uk

materials

e-steel	www.e-steel.com
Glasspages	www.glasspages.com
Plastics & Rubber Directory	www.apgate.com/plastics
Plastics News International	www.plasticsnews.com

public sector

GovCon	www.govcon.com

science

Bioresearch Online	www.bioresearchonline.com
Drug Discovery Online	www.drugdiscoveryonline.com
Laboratory Network.com	www.laboratorynetwork.com

services

HR Hub.com	www.hrhub.com
Logistics Online	www.logisticsonline.com
Purchasing Network.com	www.purchasingnetwork.com

surplus goods

Business-Auctions.com	www.business-auctions.com
ComAuction	www.comauction.com
DoveBid	www.dovebid.com
eBay Business Exchange	http://pages.ebay.com/business_exchange

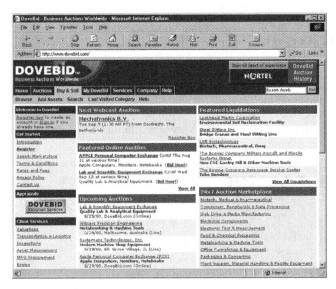

Figure 7.16 DoveBid is a central business auction site

GPbid	www.gpbid.com
HotBizNet	www.hotbiznet.com
Inventory Depot	www.inventorydepot.com
Liquidation.com	www.liquidation.com
Mondus	www.Mondus.com
MSN bCentral Auction	http://auctions.bcentral.com
Office.com	http://auctions.office.com
PatentAuction.com	www.patentauction.com
IDXMart.com	www.idxmart.com
iMark.com	www.imark.com
Industrial Assets	www.industrialassets.com
Industry Deals	www.industrydeals.com
BizSurplus	www.bizsurplus.com
DoveBid	www.dovebid.com
iMARK.com	www.imark.com
OpenSite	www.opensite.com
SupplierMarket.com	www.suppliermarket.com
SurplusBin	www.surplusbin.com
TradeOut	www.tradeout.com
Worth Guide	www.worthguide.com

office supplies

You can use the Web to furnish a new office, buy a new chair or simply place your monthly order for pens, stationery and other office supplies. Some of the online shops are online branches of established mail-order suppliers such as Neat Ideas and Viking. Others provide complete Web access to office shops, such as Staples and Office Depot. In most cases, you will find it more convenient to browse catalogues online rather than visiting a shop and discover that the prices at a Web shop include special price deals undercutting even mail-order catalogues.

In addition to standard office supplies, you can now manage all your back-office requirements online, including postage and courier delivery. The US has taken the lead in electronic postage, providing secure ways to buy and print out your own stamps or order and update your franking machine. And if you want to send urgent packages by courier, you can order the pickup and then, importantly, track your package through some of the most sophisticated database applications running on the Web. FedEx, UPS and DHL all provide direct access to their central tracking database using the Web – in some cases you can even view the signature of the recipient on their website.

If you want new telephone equipment – from a mobile phone to the latest PBX exchange – you will find that highly competitive suppliers have set up shop on the Web. Some of the major sites, such as mobile phone supplier Carphone Warehouse, let you compare tariffs and help you choose the best plan before buying a matching phone.

The Internet also provides a low-cost method for communication with Net-based telephones. Buy a special handset and a sound card for your computer and you can dial up and talk to any standard telephone, using the Internet to carry your voice. You only pay the local dial-up telephone charge to your ISP, rather than the long-distance call rate charged by a telephone company. There are systems for individuals and for companies – both providing cost savings for international calls.

equipment and furniture

Figure 8.1 Stylish office furniture and ultra-hip chairs from Herman Miller

Ashfields	www.ashfields.com
Better Buys for Business	www.betterbuys.com
Buyers Zone	www.buysmart.com
Center for Office Technology	www.cot.org
Exchange & Mart	www.exchangeandmart.co.uk
Herman Miller	www.hermanmiller.com
Neat Ideas	www.neat-ideas.com
Office Depot	www.officedepot.com
Office Products	www.officeproducts.com

The Office Shop	www.owa.co.uk
Small Office	www.smalloffice.com
Staples	www.staples.com
Turnstone Furniture	www.turnstonefurniture.com
Viking Direct	www.viking-direct.co.uk

stationery

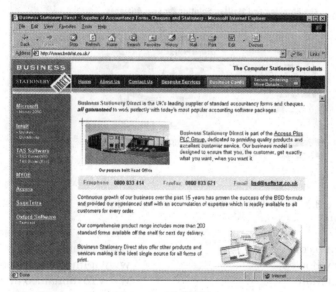

Figure 8.2   Stock up on stationery with BSD

Business Stationery Direct	www.bsdstat.co.uk
Buy.co.uk	www.buy.co.uk
EcoIreland	www.ecoireland.com
Kall-Kwik Printing (UK) Ltd	www.kallkwik.co.uk
Prontaprint	www.prontaprint.co.uk
Multiquotes	www.multiquotes.co.uk
Stamps Direct	www.rubber-stamps.co.uk
Stat Plus	www.statplus.co.uk
The Green Stationery Company	www.greenstat.co.uk

postage

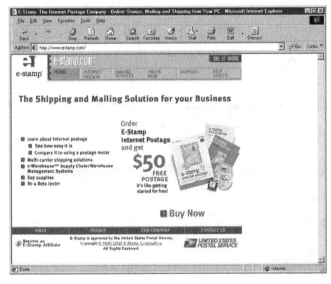

Figure 8.3 Forget the franking machine, print your own stamps with e-stamp

e-stamp.com	www.estamp.com
Pitney Bowes	www.pitneybowes.com
Royal Mail	www.royalmail.co.uk
Stamps.com	www.stamps.com
United States Postal Service (USPS)	www.usps.com

courier companies

City Link	www.city-link.co.uk
DHL	www.dhl.co.uk
Federal Express	www.fedex.com
Parcel Force	www.parcelforce.co.uk

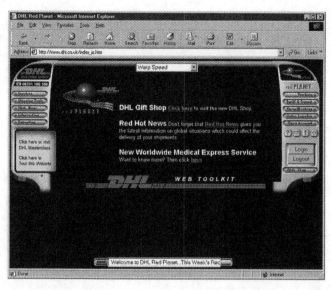

Figure 8.4 Track parcels and check the recipient's signature from the DHL website

Securicor-Omega   www.securicor.co.uk
TNT   www.tnt.co.uk
UPS   www.ups.com

telephones

BT Shop   www.btshop.bt.com
buy.co.uk   www.buy.co.uk
Call2.com   www.call2.com
Cambridge ISDN   www.cambridge-isdn.com
Carphone Warehouse   www.carphonewarehouse.com
Cellnet   www.cellnet.co.uk
Cheaper Calls UK   http://cheapercalls.8m.com
Future Numbers   www.future-numbers.co.uk
Miah Telecom   www.miah-telecom.co.uk
Mobile Bargains   www.mobilebargains.com

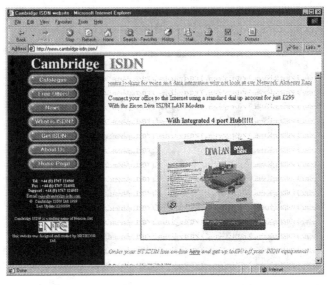

Figure 8.5 Integrate your phone system and Internet access with kit from Cambridge ISDN

One2One	www.one2one.co.uk
Orange	www.orange.co.uk
Sagem Online	www.sagem-online.com
TalkingShop	www.talkingshop.co.uk
Virgin Mobile	www.virgin.com/mobile/
Vodafone	www.vodafone-retail.co.uk

telephone over the Internet

CuSeeMe	www.cuseeme.com
Internet Telephone	www.vocaltec.com
Net2Phone	www.net2phone.com
Netmeeting	www.microsoft.com

computer equipment

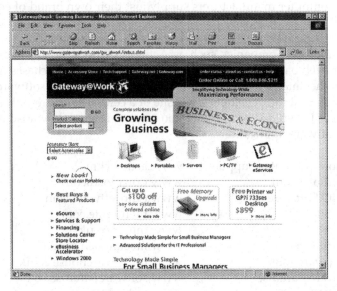

Figure 8.6 Gateway lets you create your custom computer online, then place the order

All the major computer manufacturers have online shops where you can build a computer to your specification – adding extra hard-disk capacity, a better monitor or multimedia extra. Your order is processed online and the custom-built computer delivered within a few days.

Apple Store	www.apple.com
DELL	www.dell.co.uk
Elonex	www.elonex.co.uk
Evesham Micros	www.evesham.com
Gateway 2000	www.gw2k.com
Viglen	www.viglen.co.uk

computer suppliers

The computer manufacturers supply just their own brand of equipment, but for the widest choice of computers, peripherals, accessories and software use one of the vast online computer supply superstores. Companies such as Action list thousands of items on their Web-based shop – with special discounts for purchases made over the Internet. And if you want to buy and use software instantly, visit the developer's website or a central software-only shop such as Download.com, where you can pay for and download original software applications.

Action Computer Supplies	www.action.com
Download.com	www.download.com
ECHO Software	www.echosoftware.com
Free Site	www.thefreesite.com
Inmac	www.inmac.co.uk
Macintouch	www.macintouch.com
Microwarehouse	www.microwarehouse.co.uk
Software Paradise	www.softwareparadise.co.uk
TechWeb	www.technweb.com

shareware libraries

In addition to the wide range of commercial software available, there are thousands of applications written and sold on a shareware basis: you can download and try out the software for free; if you like the product, you pay a license fee to continue using it. The most convenient places to find shareware are the following vast libraries of programs that you can download.

CNET	www.cnet.com
Rocketdownload.com	www.rocketdownload.com
TUCOWS network	www.tucows.com
WinFiles	www.winfiles.com

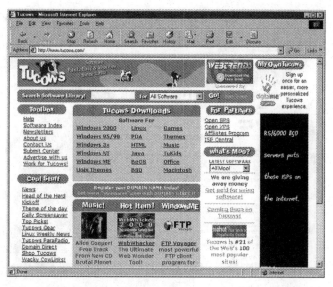

Figure 8.7 TUCOWS includes a rating scheme to help you find the best shareware software

computer support

Computers do, occasionally, go wrong – often at the most inconvenient times. If you are working in a large company, you might have a technical-support department, which can fix your computer within minutes. Alternatively, you can take out a warranty when you buy your computer – and it is worth ensuring that you have a same-day call-out option or you will be stranded for days without a computer. To help prevent problems before they occur, you can use one of these specialist support sites that can analyse your computer over the Net and tell you if there are any potential problems lurking.

Aveo	www.aveo.com
CNET	www.cnet.com
DriverZone	www.driverzone.com
Help	www.free-help.com

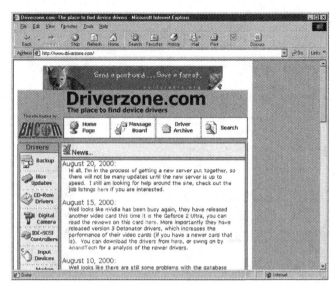

Figure 8.8 Use DriverZone to make sure that your drivers are up-to-date and avoid potential problems

MacFixIt	www.macfixit.com
SquareOneTech	www.squareonetech.com
Updates	www.updates.com
Windows Annoyances	www.annoyances.org

offices and property

The Internet promised a virtual working environment, with a scenario of home-based workers meeting in cyberspace to conduct meetings and discuss business. The reality is that a few companies can use the Net to offer some jobs to teleworkers, but everyone still works from a traditional office; even the latest Net-based start-ups need a real office space in which to base their teams of editors, designers and programmers.

The Internet can help you in the often time-consuming and frustrating job of finding an office space. Almost every commercial estate agent and chartered surveyor (who deals with commercial property) has a website with details of their services. And many of the agents now include a database of property currently available on their books.

Instead of visiting each agent's website, you could use a central database of commercial property such as Commercial Property Database or London Office Guide. These gather details from a limited range of agents and let you scan hundreds of offices across the country.

The alternative to your own leased office is to use a business centre rented on a monthly (or sometimes even weekly) basis. There are dozens of small companies spread across the country, each offering one or two locations of suites of offices for rent. The InstantOffices database gathers together a wide range of these independent companies to provide a nationwide directory of offices on offer, or you could use an international operator such as Regus.

commercial property

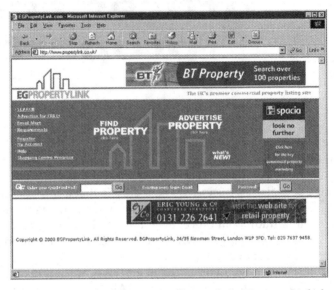

Figure 9.1 Save time finding a new office with the PropertyLink database of commercial property on offer

Adlers	www.adlers.co.uk
AICPC	www.webexpress.co.uk/aicpc
Baker Lorenz	www.bakerlorenz.co.uk
Chesterton	www.chesterton.co.uk
Commercial Network	www.tcnre.com
Commercial Properties	www.euroyellowpages.com/journals
Commercial Property Database	www.cpd.co.uk/
Commercial Property	www.cponline.co.uk
Country Estates – Commercial	www.webexpress.co.uk/countryestates
Daltons Web	www.daltons.co.uk

DTZ United Kingdom	www.dtz.se/uk
FPD Savills	www.fpdsavills.co.uk
Healey Baker	www.healey-baker.com
John D Wood	www.johndwood.co.uk
LondonOfficeGuide	www.london-office-guide.co.uk
Oxfordshire Commercial Property	www.oxonprop.co.uk
Patmore Commercial – Office Search UK	www.office-search.co.uk
Property Centre	www.property-centre.co.uk
Property Databases	www.uk-property.co.uk
Property Finder	www.propertyfinder.co.uk
Property Link	www.propertylink.co.uk
Property Market	www.property-market.co.uk
PropShop	www.dmcsoft.com/propshop/
Savoy Stewart	www.savoys.co.uk
Strutt & Parker Commercial	www.struttandparker.co.uk/ commercial

serviced offices

East West Business Centres	www.london-office.co.uk
Emerson Executive Offices	www.serviced-offices.co.uk
Fenchurch Estates Ltd	www.fenchurch.co.uk
Harvard Managed Offices	www.harvardoffices.co.uk
InstantOffices	www.instantoffices.co.uk
MWB Business Exchange	www.mwb.co.uk
Regus	www.regus.com
Westmead Business Group	www.airport-house.co.uk
Workspace Group	www.workspace-group.ltd.uk

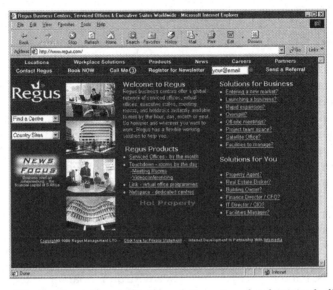

Figure 9.2 For short-term or flexible solutions, try a local serviced office or an international chain like Regus

financial management

The Internet now provides the way to access your bank account details, transfer money, pay bills, even organise insurance, pensions and credit cards. Almost every major business bank provides Internet access for their clients, giving you direct, secure access to your company's current account.

If you want to open a new business account, the bank is certain to ask you to visit the branch to explain your strategy, go through your business plan and organise an overdraft. You then need to sign paperwork before you can access the account – but from now on, with the exception of the occasional visit from the manager, you can carry out almost all your transactions over the Net.

The Web includes directories of specialists who are able to help you plan your company's financial future (or your employees' benefits, such as pensions and medical insurance). There are experts on offer with databases for hire, detailing grants available in almost every sector – provided by the government or by charitable institutions.

To keep your accounts and bank manager happy, you need to ensure that your company's cash flow is adequate. To a certain extent, this depends on your business model, but also depends on the company being paid on time – if you want to guarantee payments, you could use an invoice factoring company to manage your collections (for a fee); and if you want to grow and expand, look to the specialist business loan and venture-capital companies. All are online and all let you research and understand what is on offer before you speak to a salesperson.

business banking

Find your nearest bank from this list or use the comprehensive database of banks online around the world at AAAdir Directory (www.aaadir.com) or the similar, but wider-ranging site, Mark Bernkopf's Central Banking Resource (www.adams.patriot.net/~bernkopf/).

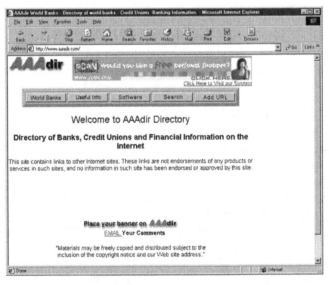

Figure 10.1 Find the website of almost any bank online from the AAAdir directory site

Adelaide Bank	www.adelaidebank.com.au
Allied Irish Bank	www.aib.ie
Bank of America	www.bankofamerica.com
Bank of England	www.bankofengland.co.uk
Bank of Melbourne	www.bankmelb.com.au
The Bank of New York	www.bankofny.com
Bank of Scotland	www.bankofscotland.co.uk/business/

Barclays Business Banking	www.business.barclays.co.uk
Chase Manhattan Bank	www.chase.com
Citibank	www.citibank.com/uk/
Co-operative Bank	www.co-operativebank.co.uk
Federal Reserve	www.federalreserve.gov
Girobank	www.girobank.co.uk
HSBC Group	www.hsbcgroup.com
Lloyds TSB	www.lloydstsb.co.uk
NatWest	www.natwest.co.uk
Reserve Bank of Australia	www.rba.gov.au/
Royal Bank of Scotland	www.rbos.co.uk
South African Reserve Bank	www.resbank.co.za
Standard Chartered Bank	www.stanchart.com
Ulster Bank Group	www.ulsterbank.com
Wells Fargo	www.wellsfargo.com

invoice factoring

Alex Lawrie	www.alexlawrie.com
Anders Financial	www.anderfinancial.co.uk
Associated Risk Consultants	www.riskconsult.co.uk
Bank of New York Co	www.bankofny.com
Credit and Debt Collection	www.insolvency.co.uk/credit
Credit Lyonnais Commercial Finance Ltd.	www.clcf.co.uk
Gaelic Invoice Factors Ltd.	www.gaelic-factors.co.uk
Griffin Services	www.griffincs.co.uk

bankruptcy advice

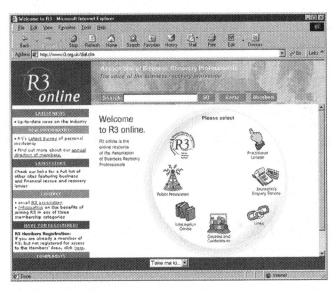

Figure 10.2 Good advice when times are bad, from the official UK society

About.com	credit.about.com/finance/credit/ mbody.htm
Association of Business Recovery Professionals	www.r3.org.uk
Bankruptcy FAQ	www.agin.com/bkfaq/
Bankruptcy Terms	www.abiworld.org/media/terms.html
Credit.com	www.credit.com
InterNet Bankruptcy Library	www.bankrupt.com
Insolvency Databases & Legal Notices	www.insolvency.com/uk/database.htm
Insolvency UK	www.insolvency.co.uk
Society of Practitioners of Insolvency	www.insolvency.org.uk

bankruptcy specialists

Alex Lawrie	www.alex-lawrie.com
Associated Risk Consultants	www.riskconsult.co.uk
Begbies Traynor	www.begbies.com
Business Credit Management UK	www.creditman.co.uk
Capital Management Ltd.	www.itac.demon.co.uk/capman
Continental Cash Collections Limited	www.cccltd.co.uk
Credit to Cash	www.ctoc.co.uk
Denton Hall	www.dentonhall.com
EULER Trade Indemnity	www.tradeindemnity.com
Equifax	www.infocheck.co.uk
Fairchild Clerk & Bloomberg	http://biznet.maximizer.com/fairchild
Fitch IBCA	www.fitchibca.com
Graydon UK	www.graydon.co.uk
IFCAS	www.ifcas.com
INSOL International	www.insol.org
Irwin Mitchell Solicitors	www.irwinmitchell.co.uk
MacDonald Partnership, The	www.tmp.co.uk
Morley & Scott	www.morleyandscott.co.uk
NCM Group	www.ncmgroup.com
O'Hara & Co.	www.ohara.co.uk
Recovery & Financial Services Ltd	www.recoveryfinancial.co.uk

business loans and finance

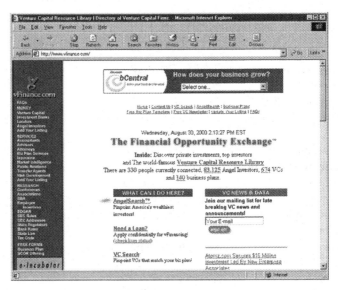

Figure 10.3 Jump-start your new company with venture capital; use the Venture Capital Resource site to find potential backers

Bank Rate Monitor	www.bankrate.com
EquipmentLeasing.com	www.equipmentleasing.com
Find.co.uk	www.find.co.uk
iii (interactive investor international)	www.iii.co.uk
GE Capital	www.ge.com/capital/smallbiz/ financial.htm
IBM Financing	www.ibm.com/financing/
LeaseAdvisor	www.leaseadvisor.com
LiveCapital	www.livecapital.com
vCapital	www.vcapital.com
Venture Capital Resources	www.vfinance.com
Venture-Capitalist.com	www.venture-capitalist.com
Merrill Lynch	http://businesscenter.ml.com

Autobytel car loans   www.autobytel.co.uk
Salomon Smith Barney   www.salomonsmithbarney.com/
       prod_svc/business/
3i Corporate finance   www.3i.com
NatWest Acquisition   www.nwacqfin.com
    Finance

grants

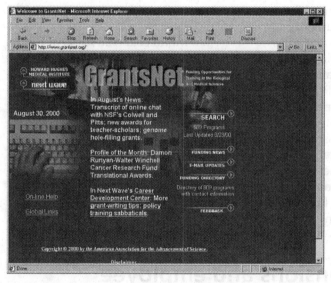

Figure 10.4 There are thousands of grants available to small businesses –
use GrantsNet to help find one suitable for your company

1066 Enterprise   www.1066.sussexenterprise.co.uk/
       grants.htm
Alfred P. Sloan   www.sloan.org
    Foundation
Combined Heat and   www.chpa.co.uk
    Power Association
Eurofi   www.eurofi.co.uk

GrantsNet   www.grantsnet.org
The Harrison   www.thp.uk.com
   Partnership
IREX   www.irex.org/

financial advisors

Choosing a Financial   http://financialplan.about.com/library/
   Planner   weekly/aa062399.htm
Financial Services   www.sib.co.uk
   Authority
Find   www.find.co.uk/advice/AIFA.html
Finding a Financial   www.planningpaysoff.org
   Planner
IFA Promotion   www.ifap.org.uk
Independent Financial   www.ifaa.org.uk
   Advisers
   Association
Interactive Investor   www.iii.co.uk/advice/
MoneyeXtra   www.moneyextra.co.uk
National Association   www.napfa.org
   of Professional
   Financial Planners

pensions and employee retirement guides

The 401(k)   www.the401k.com
The 401(k) 15-second   http://401kcenter.com/summary.htm
   summary
Blay's Guides   www.blays.co.uk
DSS (Department of   www.dss.gov.uk
   Social Security)
FIND   www.find.co.uk

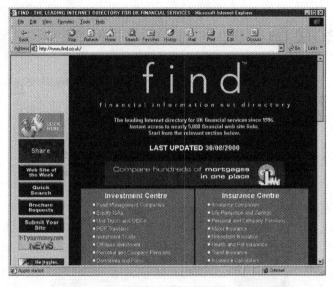

Figure 10.5 Use the central FIND directory to find local financial and pension guides and specialists

Micropal   www.micropal.com
MoneyeXtra   www.moneyextra.com

pension companies

Clerical Medical   www.clericalmedical.co.uk
The Equitable Life   www.equitable.co.uk
Friends Provident   www.friendsprovident.co.uk
Legal & General   www.landg.com
National & Mutual   www.nationalmutual.co.uk
Norwich Union   www.norwich-union.co.uk
Prudential   www.prudential.co.uk
Royal Liver Insurance www.royal-liver.com
Scottish Widows   www.scottishwidows.co.uk
Standard Life   www.standardlife.co.uk
Virgin Direct   www.virgin-direct.co.uk

credit cards

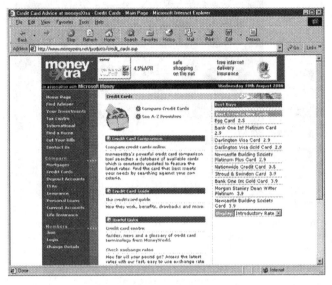

Figure 10.6 Make sure that your company credit cards have the lowest rates with MoneyeXtra

Use the Internet to compare the rates from dozens of different suppliers with specialist tools such as at MoneyeXtra (www.moneyextra.co.uk/products/credit_cards.asp) – and make sure that your company's cards are not the most expensive on offer.

AmericanExpress	www.americanexpress.com
Aria	www.aria.com
BankOne	www.bankone-uk.com
CapitalOne	www.capitalone.co.uk
Charity Credit Card	www.charitycard.co.uk
DinersClub	www.dinersclub.com
Egg	www.egg.com
Goldfish	www.goldfish.com
i-Circle	www.icircle.co.uk

Marbles	www.getmarbles.co.uk
MasterCard	www.mastercard.com
Moneynet	www.moneynet.co.uk
Novus	www.novusnet.com
Visa	www.visa.com

insurance:
office, liability and general

Ault Insurance Brokers	www.jsault.demon.co.uk
Axa Direct	www.axa.co.uk
Ben McArdle	www.benmcardle.ie/
British Insurance & Investment Broker's Association	www.biiba.org.uk
Business Insurance Online	www.businessinsurance.com
Chatburns	www.chatburns.co.uk
Churchill Insurance	www.churchill.co.uk
CIC Insurance	www.cicinsurance.co.uk
Cornhill Direct	www.cornhilldirect.co.uk
Eagle Star Insurance	www.eaglestardirect.co.uk
FIND	www.find.co.uk
Hill House Hammond	www.hhh.co.uk
iii (Interactive Investor International)	www.iii.co.uk
Insurance Online	www.insure.net
MoneyeXtra	www.moneyextra.co.uk
Moody's Investors Service	www.moodys.com/insurance
National Association of Insurance Commissioners	www.naic.org
Royal & Sun Alliance	www.royal-and-sunalliance.com
Screen Trade	www.screentrade.co.uk
The Insurance News Network	www.insure.com
Yahoo! Insurance	http://insurance.yahoo.com

motor insurance

The AA	www.theaa.com
Admiral	www.admiral.uk.com
autobytel.co.uk	www.autobytel.co.uk
Belair Direct	www.belairdirect.com
Carsource	www.carsource.co.uk
CGU Direct	www.cgu-direct.co.uk
Cornhill Direct	www.cornhilldirect.co.uk/van
GEICO	www.geico.com
Insure.com	www.insure.com/auto
Ironsure	www.ironsure.com
Norwich Union Direct	www.norwichunion.co.uk
Privilege Insurance	www.privilege.co.uk
Pru Auto Discounts	www.prudential.com/insurance/auto
WhatCar?	www.whatcar.co.uk

medical insurance

About.com – Health Care Industry	http://healthcare.about.com
Aetna US Healthcare	www.aetnaushc.com
Blue Cross	www.bluecross.com
BUPA	www.bupa.co.uk
Health Plan Directory	www.healthplandirectory.com
Legal and General Healthcare	www.landg.com/health/health1.html
Medibroker	www.medibroker.co.uk
Norwich Union	www.norwich-union.co.uk
PPP	www.ppphealthcare.co.uk
XShealth	www.xshealth.co.uk

global business

The Internet offers a tempting global outlook with millions of potential customers and business partners scattered across the world. One of the most effective ways to reach this global audience is to set up a website that can be accessed easily by any customer anytime. However, your website should be translated into other languages to cater for non-native English speakers.

On the Web you can find out about doing business in another country, find and create relationships with new business partners, and follow local business etiquette to ensure you export your products and services successfully. Finally, you can find experts who can help you manage your new venture including lawyers, accountants and bankers.

One of the best places to start is the archive of reports produced by the British Council. Other government export departments often provide similar research information and these include lists of potential contacts, official requests for tender and even, as with the British Council, a daily e-mail service to keep you in touch with niche trade sectors. The exception to this rule is the US – there is little available for companies hoping to import to the US. This is because, historically, most of the Internet world centres on the US; therefore, it assumes that business people online are American and do not need this information.

You will find the Web packed with guides and advice on how to export to a particular country – often provided by the country's own government. To start your research, you should look at the official reports from the World Bank, as well as the economic sites explaining the current and future outlook for various countries. Once you have decided that a country is viable, you can use telephone directories, market research and online business guides to help choose suitable partners.

translations

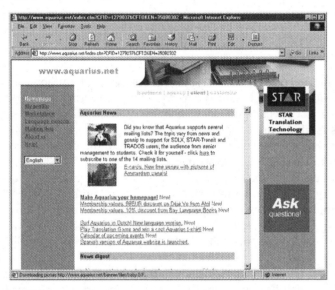

Figure 11.1   If you need a multilingual site, find a translator with Aquarius

Babelfish   http://babelfish.altavista.com
Aquarius   www.aquarius.net

general guides for export

Big Emerging Markets   www.ita.doc.gov/bems/
   Information Resource Page
British Council   www.britcoun.org

British Trade International	www.brittrade.com
Company Annual Reports On-Line (CAROL)	www.carol.co.uk
Corporate Location	www.corporatelocation.com
The Economist Intelligence Unit	www.eiu.com
Emerging Markets Companion	www.emgmkts.com
EMU Net	www.euro-emu.co.uk
Hieros Gamos/Lex Mundi Business Guides	www.hg.org/guides.html
International Monetary Fund (IMF)	www.imf.org
The Internationalist	www.internationalist.com
Statistical data locators	www.ntu.edu.sg/library/stat/statdata.htm
Worldly Investor	www.worldlyinvestor.com

world economics

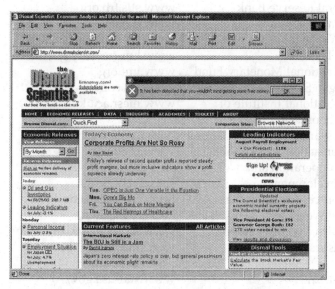

Figure 11.2   Read economic forecasts from the Dismal Scientist

Alan Greenspan	www.geocities.com/~the-igloo/greenspan/
Australia Department of Treasury	www.treasury.gov.au/
The Budget – UK	www.hm-treasury.gov.uk
American federal budget	http://w3.access.gpo.gov/usbudget/index.html
Bureau of Economic Analysis	www.bea.doc.gov/
CNNfn	www.cnnfn.com/news/economy/
Confederation of British Industry	www.cbi.org.uk
The Dismal Scientist	www.dismalscientist.com
Dr Ed Yardeni's Economics Network	www.yardeni.com
DTI (The Department of Trade and Industry)	www.dti.gov.uk
The Economist	www.economist.co.uk
The Economist Intelligence Unit	www.eiu.com
Euromoney	www.emwl.com
Federal Reserve Bank	www.stls.frb.org
Financial Times	www.ft.com
FinWeb	www.finweb.com
HM Treasury	www.hm-treasury.gov.uk
International Monetary Fund	www.imf.org
Morgan Stanley	www.ms.com
The National Institute of Economic and Social Research	www.niesr.ac.uk
Organisation for Economic Co-operation and Development	www.oecd.org
Resources for Economists on the Web	http://rfe.wustl.edu/EconFAQ.html
Scottish Executive Reports	www.scotland.gov.uk
Statistical data locators	www.ntu.edu.sg/library/statdata.htm
Stat-USA	www.stat-usa.gov/
Treasury Worldwide	www.treasuryworldwide.com

USA Today Quarterly	www.usatoday.com/money/
Economic Survey	economy/econ0001.htm
US Census Bureau	www.census.gov/cgi-bin/
	briefroom/BriefRm
The Virtual Economy	http://ve.ifs.org.uk
World Bank	www.worldbank.org

business in Europe

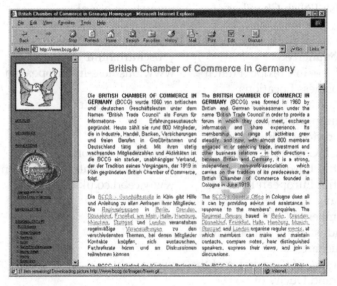

Figure 11.3 Want to do business in Germany? Get advice and contacts from the British Chamber of Commerce

Albanian World Wide Web Home Page	www.albanian.com
Athens Chamber of Commerce and Industry	www.acci.gr
Austrian Federal Economic Chamber	www.wk.or.at/aw/aw_intl/

Bank of Austria	www.austria.eu.net/oenb/english
Belgian Federal Government	www.belgium.fgov.be/en_index.htm
Belgium Business Finder	www.infospace.com/uk.tetegr/intldb/bizfindint.htm?QO=BE
Bridge to Greece and Cyprus	www.greekvillage.com/bridge/bridge.htm
Britain in the European Union	www.fco.gov.uk
British Chamber of Commerce in Germany	www.bccg.de
British Polish Chamber of Commerce	www.bccg.org.pl
British–Swedish Chamber of Commerce	www.swednet.org.uk/bscintro.html
Business in Europe: French Business Locations	www.business-in-europe.com
Central and Eastern European Business Directory (CEEBD)	www.ceebd.co.uk
British Council	www.britcoun.org
Central Europe Online	www.invest.centraleurope.com
Central European Business Daily	www.cebd.co.uk
Chamber of Commerce and Industry for Romania and Bucharest	www.ccir.ro
Chamber of Commerce of the Grand Duchy of Luxembourg	www.cc.lu
Confoederatio Helvetica	www.admin.ch/ch/e/index.html
Contact '99 – Finland Business Services	www.contactfinland.fi/business.html
Council of Europe	www.coe.fr
Croatian Chamber of Economy	www.hgk.hr
Czech Info Centre	www.muselik.com/czech/toc.html

Danish Exporters	www.danish-exporters.tele.dk
Danish Ministry of Business and Industry	www.em.dk/engvers.htm
Central Europe Online	www.centraleurope.com
HUGIN	www.huginonline.com
Doing Business in Azerbaijan	www.soros.org/azerbijan/ azerbusi.html
Soros	www.soros.org
Economic Chamber of Macedonia	www.mchamber.org.mk
Embassy of Italy in the United States	www.italyemb.org/
Romanian Embassy	www.roembus.org
Estonian Ministry of Foreign Affairs	www.vm.ee
Euro Guide	www.euroguide.org
European Business Directory	www.europages.com
Europa	www.europa.eu.int
France Business Protocol	www.worldbiz.com/ bizfrance.html
Germany Business Protocol	www.worldbiz.com/ bizgermany.html
Francexport	www.francexport.com
French Foreign Ministry	www.france.diplomatie.fr
German Federal Ministry for Foreign Affairs	www.auswaertiges-amt.de
Go-Spain Business Pages	www.go-spain.com/business
Greece Ministry of Foreign Affairs	www.mfa.gr
Hellenic Search Engine	www.robby.gr
IDA Ireland	www.idaireland.com
Interstate Statistical Committee of the Commonwealth of Independent States	www.unece.org/stats/cisstat
Invest in Finland Bureau	www.investinfinland.fi
Invest in Sweden Agency	www.isa.se
Ireland Government	www.irlgov.ie
Irish Trade Web	www.itw.ie

Ireland On-Line	http://home.iol.ie
Italian Chambers of Commerce	www.italchambers.net
Italy Foreign Minstry	www.esteri.it/eng/
Luxembourg	www.etat.lu
Netherlands Foreign Investment Agency	www.nfia.com
Portugal Ministry of Finance	www.dgep.pt
Sweden Finance Ministry	www.sb.gov.se
Tenders Electronic Daily	http://ted.eur-op.eu.int

business in North America

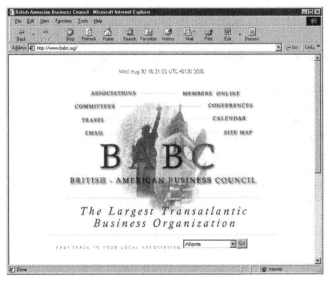

Figure 11.4 Few websites support imports into the US, but the BABC provides a good starting point for advice and information

British–American Business Council (BABC)	www.babc.org
Business Broker Web	www.business-broker.com

Canadian Commercial   www.ccc.ca
Corporation (CCC)

business in Central and South America

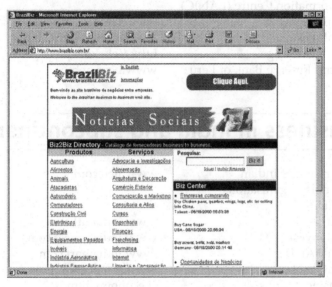

Figure 11.5   Find out about the biggest potential market in the Americas –
with BrazilBiz

AmchamNet   www.amcham.com.br
Argentina Business   www.invertir.com
Bankomext Business Centre   http://mexico.businessonline.
                                      gob.mx
Brazil Infonet   www.brazilinfo.net
BrazilBiz   www.brazilbiz.com.br
Camara Venezolano Britanica   www.britcham.com.ve
  de Comercio (CVBC)
ChileTrade.cl   www.chiletrade.cl
Chile Business Directory   www.chilnet.cl

Dominican Republic One	www.dr1.com
Guatemala Online	www.quetzalnet.com
INEGI – National Institute of Statistics, Geography and Informatics	www.inegi.gob.mx
Inter-American Development Bank Online Databases	http://database.iadb.org
Latin American Network Information Centre (LANIC)	www.lanic.utexas.edu
LatinFocus	www.latin-focus.com
LatinInvestor	www.latininvestor.com
Peru Home Page	http://ekeko.rcp.net.pe
Central Reserve Bank of Peru	www.bcrp.gob.pe

business in India and subcontinent

Federation of Indian Export Organisations (FIEO)	www.fieo.com
India	www.indiaintl.com
India Invest	www.india-invest.com
IndiaMART	www.indiamart.com
Indian Economy and Business Links	www.ib-net.com/links/economy.htm

business in the Far East

Asia Business Connection (ABC)	www.asiabiz.com
Asia Inc.	www.asia-inc.com
Asia-Pacific Economic Cooperation (APEC)	www.apecsec.org.sg
Bank of Japan	www.boj.or.jp/en/
BPS Statistics Indonesia	www.bps.go.id/

China External Trade Development Council	www.tptaiwan.org.tw/
China Infobank Limited	www.chinainfobank.com/
China Web	www.comnex.com/
China Window	http://china-window.com/
ChinaPages	www.chinapages.com
ECCP Online	www.eccp.com
Far Eastern Economic Review (FEER)	www.feer.com
Federation of Pakistan Chambers of Commerce and Industry	www.fpcci.com
Hong Kong Shipping Directory	www.info.gov.hk/mardep/ sdfiles/shipdir.htm
Hong Kong Statistics	www.info.gov.hk/censtatd/
Hong Kong Trade Development Council	www.tdctrade.com
Japan External Trade Organisation (JETRO), London	www.jetro.co.uk
Japan Financials	http://japanfinancials.com
Japan Information Network	www.jinjapan.org/stat/
Nikkei Net Interactive	www.nni.nikkei.co.jp

business in Australasia

ANZlink Limited	www.nzlink.com
Australian Business Limited	www.abol.net
Australian Chamber of Commerce and Industry	www.acci.asn.au
Doing Business in Australia	www.claytonutz.com.au/fr-bus.htm
Hints to Exporters Visiting New Zealand	www.brittrade.com/publications/ new_zealand/

business in the Middle East

Arab Net	www.arab.net
Central Bureau of Statistics – Israel	www.cbs.gov.il/engindex.htm
Dubai Internet Pages	http://dubai.uae-pages.com/business/
Egypt Corporate Information	www.corporateinformation.com/egcorp.html
Iranian Trade Association	www.iraniantrade.org
Israel Ministry of Foreign Affairs	www.israel.org/mfa
Israel Yellow Pages	www.yellowpages.co.il
Lebanon.com	www.lebanon.com

business in Africa

Africa Online	www.africaonline.co.ke
Coconet: Ivory Coast	http://africa-info.ihost.com/pages/2ci/ann0800.htm
Guyana News and Information	www.guyana.org
South Africa: i Pages	www.ipages.co.za
KenyaWeb	www.kenyaweb.com

human resources and staff

Finding new staff and managing existing human resources are to-gether one of the most time-consuming jobs for any small business. It can take several advertisements and weeks of interviews to find the right candidate for a job vacancy; once they have joined the company, you will need to spend hours poring over paperwork required by the government for their tax, national insurance and benefits.

You could cut out one stage of this process by using a recruitment agency, but they often charge 20–30 per cent of the starting salary to place someone who is on their books. Internet-based recruitment agencies work in a similar way, but as overheads are low, should charge less. Some sites let you advertise your job online free, but you will still have to interview and assess each one.

When you have a selection of applicants, you will need to test them and see how they react to your work environment. Again, the web can help with its specialist psychometric testing sites that help you devise strategies to find hardworking dedicated staff.

Once you have hired your staff, you need to put in place admin-istration and support to manage the payroll, bank transfers, benefits and so on. Some of these administrative tasks can be put out to specialist outsourcing companies, which will manage the payroll, the benefits list or the holiday schedule – using the Web. If you prefer to work on a traditional basis, you can use the Web to learn about how to look after your staff and how to deal with difficult situations such as disputes and dismissal. For advice, sample forms and paperwork, ask your accountant or visit the Institute of Personnel and Development (www.ipd.co.uk) or Law Pack publishing (www.lawpack.co.uk); in the US you can find your local state regulatory body in the WorkIndex directory (www.workindex.com).

general HR sites

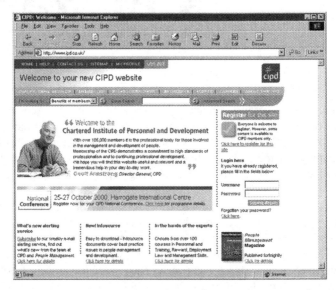

Figure 12.1 The IPD provides a great starting point for guides, advice, forms and help on hiring, firing and managing staff

Chartered Institute of Personnel and Development   www.ipd.co.uk

Official guides, advice, forms and plans to help you hire, manage and fire staff effectively include the following sites.

Training and Enterprise Councils	www.tec.co.uk
TriNET VCO	www.trinetvco.com
WorkIndex	www.workindex.com

workplace safety

American Industrial Hygiene Association	www.aiha.org
Hours of Labor and Safety	www4.law.cornell.edu/uscode/40/ ch5.html
Occupational Safety and Health	http://oshweb.me.tut.fi

staff benefits

BenefitsLink	www.benefitslink.com/index.shtml
Business and Workplace Briefs	www.nolo.com/ChunkSB/ SB.index.html
Center for Employee Ownership	www.nceo.org/
ERISA Industry Committee	www.eric.org/
Employee Benefit Plans Foundation	www.ifebp.org/
Execustaff	www.execustaff.net/
FED Net	www.fed.org/index.html
IBIS Online	www.ibisnews.com/
IOMA Newsletters	www.ioma.com/ioma/about.html
Your Rights in the Workplace	www.nolo.com/nn193.html

testing and interviews

Assess Yourself Online	www.srg.co.uk/assessyou.html
Career Mapper	www.ti.com/recruit/docs/ resume.shtml

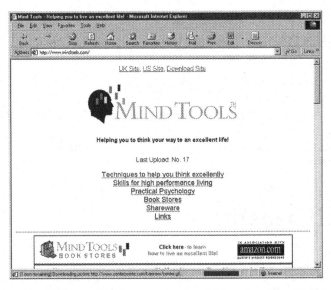

Figure 12.2 Make sure that you get the right person for the job with assessments from Mind Tools

Job Assessment   www.namss.org.uk/
                                      jobassess.htm

Mind Tools   www.mindtools.com

finding staff

BestPeople	www.bestpeople.co.uk
CareerCentral	www.careercentral.com
CareerMosaic UK	www.careermosaic-uk.co.uk
CareerZine	www.careerzine.co.uk
CreativeGroup	www.creativegroup.com
e-job	www.e-job.net
Gradunet–Virtual Careers Office	www.gradunet.co.uk
JobHunter	www.jobhunter.co.uk
Jobs Unlimited	www.jobsunlimited.co.uk
JobSearch	www.jobsearch.co.uk

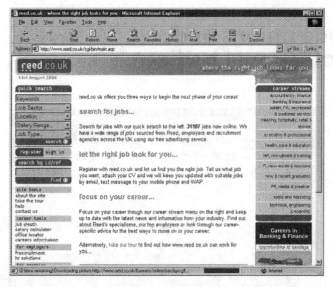

Figure 12.3 The vast high-street agency Reed lets you search its database online – or place your own classified ads

JobSite UK	www.jobsite.co.uk
Jobworld	www.jobworld.co.uk
Reed Online	www.reed.co.uk
Robert Half	www.roberthalf.com
Taps	www.taps.com

workplace illness – stress management

American Institute of Stress	www.stress.org
Stress Management	www.suite101.com
Stress Stop	www.stressstop.com
Wes Sime Stress Management	www.unl.edu/stress/

trade unions and professional bodies

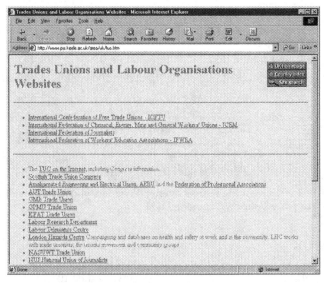

Figure 12.4 Keep in touch with the unions for your industry – find them at All Trade Unions

All Trade Unions	www.psr.keele.ac.uk/area/uk/tus.htm
Employee Relations & Trade Unions	www.nbs.ntu.ac.uk/staff/lyerj/list/hrer.htm
Equal Opportunities Commission	www.eoc.org.uk
Commonwealth Trade Union Council	www.commonwealthtuc.org
Connect	www.ste.org.uk
LabourStart UK	www.labourstart.org/uk

individual trade unions

GFTU	www.gftu.org.uk
AEEU	www.aeeu.org.uk
AMPS	www.amps.demon.co.uk
ATL	www.atl.org.uk
AUT	www.aut.org.uk
BALPA	www.balpa.org.uk
BECTU	www.bectu.org.uk
BFAWU	www.bfawu.org.uk
BMU	www.musiciansunion.org.uk
British Actors' Equity Association	www.equity.org.uk
British Dental Association	www.bda-dentistry.org.uk
CATU	www.gftu.org.uk/html/ catu_index.html
CSP	www.csphysio.org.uk
CWU	www.cwu.org
EIS	www.eis.org.uk
EMA	www.ema.org.uk
FBU	www.fbu-ho.org.uk
GFTU	www.gftu.org.uk
GMB Southern Regions	www.gmb-southern.org.uk
Graphical, Paper & Media Union	www.gpmu.org.uk
HCSA	www.hcsa.com
IPMS	www.ipms.org.uk
KFAT	www.kfat.org.uk
MSF	www.msf.org.uk
NASUWT	www.teachersunion.org.uk
NATFHE	www.natfhe.org.uk
NUDAGO	www.gftu.org.uk
NUJ	www.poptel.org.uk/nuj
NUMAST	www.numast.org
NUT	www.teachers.org.uk
OILC	www.oilc.org
PAT	www.pat.org.uk
PCS	www.pcs.org.uk

PFA	www.thepfa.co.uk
Police Federation, England & Wales	www.polfed.org.uk
RCN	www.nursing-standard.co.uk
T&G	www.tgwu.org.uk
TSSA	www.tssa.org.uk
TUC Education	www.education-online.co.uk
UNIFI	www.unifi.org.uk
UNISON	www.unison.org.uk
USDAW	www.poptel.org.uk/usdaw

news

The Internet is a perfect delivery mechanism for news. It is fast, efficient, direct and offers a full range of multimedia from TV and video clips seen on the Web to a text-based summary delivered each morning by e-mail. Some news sites provide archives of reports, stories and newspaper features that you can use for research; others deliver the latest news as it happens, direct to your computer, mobile phone or e-mail account.

Almost every newspaper, magazine and television station around the world now has a website and the majority offer their content free to Web-based viewers. If you can not find the paper or magazine that you want, use a search tool such as NewsRack or The Paper Boy to find its home page. You can buy *The Times* newspaper each morning or you can read the entire content (and access an archive of its content over the past few years) free using the Web.

Best of all, you can ask for highly targeted news stories. If you want a summary of news about your particular industry, your favourite football team, the local weather and portfolio of stocks you hold, that is not a problem. Use a site such as InfoBeat to define your own customised newspaper sent by e-mail.

news digests

CEO Express   www.ceoexpress.com
InfoBeat   www.infobeat.com

Figure 13.1 InfoBeat will deliver a daily custom newspaper by e-mail

finding news websites

Newsrack	www.newsrack.com
Paperboy	www.thepaperboy.com
Worldwide News	www.worldwidenews.com

general news

BBC News/Business	http://news.bbc.co.uk/hi/english/ business/
NewsAlert	www.newsalert.com
Newswatch	www.newswatch.co.uk
Time	www.time.com

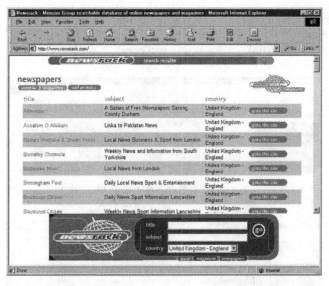

Figure 13.2 Trying to find a magazine or newspaper? Use Newsrack

business news

ABC News	www.abcnews.com/sections/business/
Advanced Financial Network	www.advfn.com
AFX News	www.afxnews.com
CBS.MarketWatch	http://cbs.marketwatch.com
CNBC Europe	www.cnbceurope.com
CNNfn	www.cnnfn.com
Financial Times	www.ft.com
Fox Market Wire	www.foxmarketwire.com
MSNBC	www.msnbc.com
The New York Times: business	www.nytimes.com/business
Reuters MoneyNet	www.moneynet.com
TheStreet.com	www.thestreet.com
SiliconValley	www.siliconvalley.com
UK Business Park	www.ukbusinesspark.co.uk

Weekend City Press Review	www.news-review.co.uk
Wall Street Journal	www.wsj.com

Figure 13.3 The *Financial Times* provides a vast resource of daily and archived business and financial news

country-specific news

Agence France Presse	www.afp.com
Anorak	www.anorak.co.uk
CBS Marketwatch	www.cbsmarketwatch.com
China Daily	www.chinadaily.net
China News Digest	www.cnd.org
Crayon	www.crayon.net
The Christian Science Monitor	www.csmonitor.com
Euromoney Online	www.emwl.com
Financial Times	www.ft.com
InfoBeat	www.infobeat.com

International Herald Tribune	www.iht.com
Japan Press Network	www.jpn.co.jp
Kidon Media Link	www.kidon.com/media-link/
The Nando Times	www.nando.net
The New York Times	www.nytimes.com
NewsNow	www.newsnow.co.uk
NewsPage	www.newspage.com
Press Association	www.pa.press.net
Reuters	www.reuters.com
World News	www.wn.com

business magazines

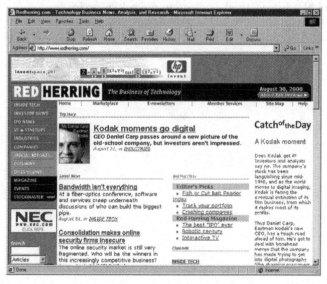

Figure 13.4 Red Herring chronicles the news from high-tech companies and start-ups

Accountancy Age	www.accountancyage.co.uk
Accountancy Magazine	www.accountancymagazine.com
The Banker	www.thebanker.com

The Bankers' Almanac	www.bankersalmanac.com
Banking and Technology News Service Network	www.btnsn.com
BBC Online Business	http://news.bbc.co.uk/hi/english/ business/
Brill's Content	www.brillscontent.com
Business 2.0	www.business2.com
Business Week Online	www.businessweek.com
The Economist	www.economist.com
Fast Company	www.fastcompany.com
Forbes	www.forbes.com
Fortune	www.fortune.com
Inc. Online	www.inc.com
The Industry Standard	www.thestandard.com
Marketing Week Online	www.marketing-week.co.uk
Nikkei Net Interactive	www.nni.nikkei.co.jp
Red Herring	www.redherring.com

reference and research

The Internet can transform the way in which you plan and research your next campaign. It provides a vast library of often free reference material that can help you find out about a new market, check the existing competition and then plan to make the right decisions. It is a great reference tool for marketing, sales, product development, market-place research and customer feedback. The one drawback is information overload – because the Web is so vast, with over one billion pages of information, it is very easy to get lost or simply waste time trying to find the information you need. However, if you look on the Web, you will find encyclopaedias, dictionaries, telephone directories, maps, statistical research, government reports and company information.

The Internet is packed with statistical data, research, background information, reports, news and user-comment information – and it can all be searched for free. Some websites will charge you for their information (normally specialist information such as company credit ratings or focus group meetings), but almost all the other sources of information are free to access. Much of what is written online is submitted by reputable companies, journalists and commentators. Unfortunately, all information is equal online, so you will come across as many wild theories of first-year students as sage words from respected management gurus.

general reference

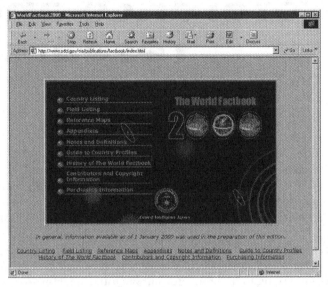

Figure 14.1 Check your facts with the CIA Worldbook

About.com	www.about.com
Argus Clearinghouse	www.clearinghouse.net
CIA Worldbook	www.odci.gov/cia/publications/ factbook/
refdesk.com	www.refdesk.com
Reference.com	www.reference.com
Yahoo! Reference	http://dir.yahoo.com/reference/

dictionaries and encyclopaedias

A Web of On-line Dictionaries	www.facstaff.bucknell.edu/ rbeard/diction.html
AltaVista – Translations	http://babelfish.altavista.com

Encarta	www.encarta.com
Encyclopedia.com	www.encyclopedia.com
Encyclopaedia Britannica	www.eb.com
Merriam Webster	www.m-w.com

questions answered

Ask an expert	www.askanexpert.com
Ask Jeeves!	www.askjeeves.com
Information Please	www.infoplease.com
The Why Files	http://whyfiles.news.wisc.edu/
Xplore	www.xplore.com

local information

County Web	www.countyweb.co.uk
DETR – Local Government	www.local.doe.gov.uk
Scoot	www.scoot.co.uk
Town Pages	www.townpages.co.uk

yellow pages

Everyone uses the *Yellow Pages* – now it is online and fully indexed; great for business to business or personal users who want to find a business.

Australia	www.yellowpages.com.au
Canada	www.canadayellowpages.com
New Zealand	www.yellowpages.co.nz
South Africa	www.easyinfo.co.za
UK	www.yell.co.uk
USA	www.bigyellow.com.

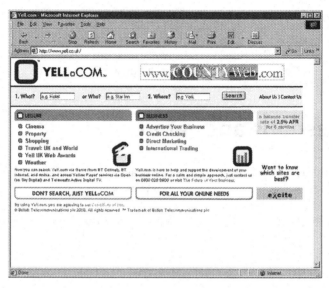

Figure 14.2 Yellow Pages are invaluable – and even better online

government information

10 Downing Street	www.number-10.gov.uk
Department of Commerce	www.doc.gov
Department of Labor	www.dol.gov
Department of the Treasury	www.ustreas.gov
Department of Trade and Industry (UK)	www.dti.gov.uk
Foreign Office	www.fco.gov.uk
Governments on the WWW	www.gksoft.com/govt/
HM Treasury	www.hm-treasury.gov.uk

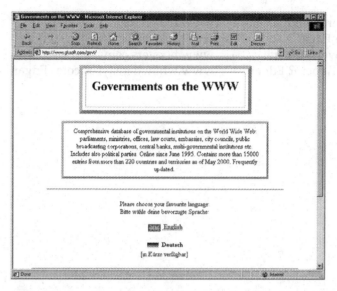

Figure 14.3 Use governments on the WWW to find a government or department online

company research

The Net can give you access to the official annual reports filed by all registered companies. In the UK, companies file their annual reports at Companies House (www.companies-house.gov.uk). Visit their website to request a copy of their accounts or use a company such as Dun & Bradstreet (www.dunandbrad.co.uk) for a fee-based credit report on the company. The US equivalent is EDGAR, which offers a more detailed report and includes public share offers and bankruptcy – and best of all, on the Web you can view them for free.

Companies Online	www.companiesonline.com
Company Sleuth	www.companysleuth.com
Dialog	www.dialog.com
Dun & Bradstreet	www.dunandbrad.co.uk

Federal Filings Online	www.fedfil.com
Free Edgar	www.freeedgar.com
Hoover's Online	www.hoovers.com
WhoWhere? Edgar	www.whowhere.lycos.com/Edgar/

sales and marketing

The Internet has truly revolutionised the world of sales and marketing. The Web provides relatively easy access to a potential audience of hundreds of millions of users, e-mail offers a fast, low-cost and effective direct route to an individual, and even display advertising has seen a shift away from glossy magazines to small banner ads on commercial websites.

If you want to research a new way of marketing, there are sites providing guides and advice; if you are starting up and have little or no experience of what works in sales and marketing, you will find the starter sections of the general marketing sites, such as Inc. and bCentral, useful. Alternatively, turn to a specialist site from a consultant offering free advice (in the hope of a paid job) about online marketing or export sales or their particular expert subject.

If you are looking for ways to implement a marketing campaign, the Web has online suppliers that can sell you almost any personalised promotional gizmo or manage printing and delivery, party balloons or hiring a guest speaker for a product launch.

Perhaps the obvious way to reach the new global audience is to send out a million e-mails to unsuspecting users, promoting your new widget. Don't – you will get flamed with hate mail and damage your company's reputation. Make sure that you only use lists from one of the reputable suppliers. You will also find good advice on many business portals (page 2) and from professional organisations such as the DMA (www.the-dma.com).

The Web can help you streamline your relations with the press – specialist agencies can send out press releases to thousands of journalists around the world selected by niche speciality. Or you can use the Net to help with direct consumer feedback. One of the latest tools for marketing research is online focus groups, such as Greenfield Online, which let you submit your product plans or designs to a panel of tens, hundreds or thousands of online research subjects – you get feedback within minutes and at a far lower cost than traditional forums.

general E-marketing information

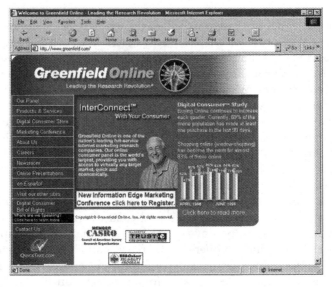

Figure 15.1 Greenfield Online helps provide Web-based consumer testing services

Advertising Association	www.adassoc.org.uk
American Marketing Association	www.ama.org
American Small Business Association	www.salesdoctors.com/directory/dircos/
bCentral	www.bcentral.com

Business 2.0   www.business2.com
DoubleClick   www.doubleclick.net
Fast Company   www.fastcompany.com
Greenfield Online   www.greenfield.com
Guerrilla Marketing Online www.gmarketing.com
Inc.   www.inc.com
More Business   www.morebusiness.com
Wilson Internet Services www.wilsonweb.com

direct mail and e-mail

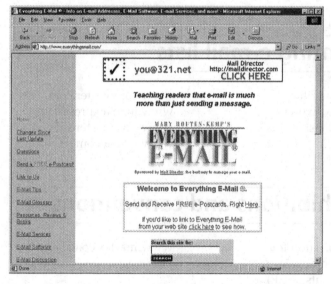

Figure 15.2   Want to find out about e-mail – use EverythingE-mail

Alphasoft   www.alphasoftware.com
Arial Software Campaign   www.arialsoftware.com
Colorado Soft WorldMerge   www.coloradosoft.com
Direct Email List Source   www.copywriter.com/lists/
Direct Email Marketing   www.e-target.com
Direct Marketing Association www.the-dma.com

Direct Marketing News	www.dmnews.com
Direct Marketing Club of Southern California	www.dmcsc.com
ELetter	www.eletter.com
EverythingE-mail	www.everythingemail.com
infoUSA	www.infousa.com
Interact	www.interact.com
MailKing	www.mailking.com
Mailing-Labels	www.mailing-labels.com
ListsNow	www.listsnow.com/uk/
Stamps.com	www.stamps.com
Yahoo!	www.yahoo.com:companies:direct marketing:email marketing

renting e-mail lists

Copywriter	www.copywriter.com/lists
InBox Express	www.inboxexpress.com
PostMasterDirect	www.postmasterdirect.com
Targ-it	www.targ-it.com

exhibitions and conventions

Association for Conferences & Events (ACE)	www.martex.co.uk/ace
British Association of Conference Destinations	www.bacd.org.uk
Exhibition Venues Association (EVA)	www.martex.co.uk/eva
Celebrity Speakers International	www.speakers.co.uk
Exhibit Connections	www.exhibit-connections.com

Figure 15.3 Get a celebrity to open your next convention – from Celebrity Speakers

Exhibitions and Displays Direct	www.exhibitions-displays.co.uk
Exhibitions round the world	www.exhibitions-world.com
Expobase	www.expobase.com
ExpoWeb	www.expoweb.com
Trade Show Exhibits	www.tradegroup.com
Venue Directory	www.venuedirectory.com
Yahoo! Conventions and Trade Shows	http://uk.dir.yahoo.com/ Business_and_Economy/Companies/ Conventions_and_Trade_Shows/

conference centres

Aberdeen Exhibition & Conference Centre	www.aecc.co.uk

Albert Hall Conference Centre	www.confnottingham.co.uk
Alexandra Palace	www.alexandrapalace.com
Barbicon Centre	www.barbican.org.uk
Bournemouth International Centre (BIC)	www.bournemouth.gov.uk/bic
Business Design Centre	www.business-design-centre.com
Cardiff International Arena & Convention Centre	http://homer.cwtc.co.uk
Earls Court Olympia	www.eco.co.uk
Edinburgh International Conference Centre	www.eicc.co.uk
Harrogate International Centre	www.harrogateinternational centre.co.uk
London Arena	www.londonarena.co.uk
Manchester Conference Centre	www.meeting.co.uk
National Exhibition Centre	www.necgroup.co.uk/nec
Queen Elizabeth II Conference Centre	www.qeiicc.co.uk
Royal Horticultural Halls & Conference Centre	www.horticultural-halls.co.uk

promotional materials

Accolade	www.accolade.uk.com
B-loony	www.b-loony.co.uk
Castelli Diaries	www.castelli.co.uk
Mousemats	www.mousemats-r-us.com
Promotional World	www.netcomuk.co.uk/~pukka/ promotion.html
Salesbuilders	www.salesbuilders.co.uk
Yahoo! Promotional Items	http://uk.dir.yahoo.com/ Business_and_Economy/Companies/ Marketing_and_Advertising/ Advertising/Promotional_Items/

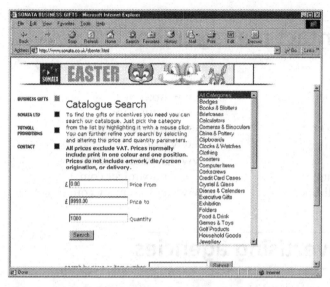

Figure 15.4 Salesbuilders supplies promotional material to help build your brand sales

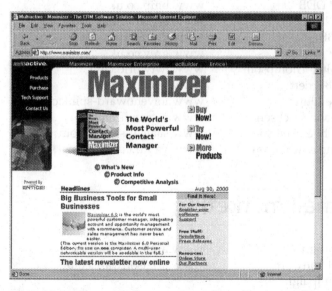

Figure 15.5 Make the most of your contact list with a specialist contact management program

contact management

Palm	www.palm.com
HewlettPackard	www.hp.com
Lotus	www.lotus.com
Microsoft	www.microsoft.com
Psion	www.psion.com
ACT!	www.symantec.com
Maximizer	www.maximizer.com
GoldMine	www.goldminesw.com

advertising agencies

Abbott Mead Vickers	www.amvbbdo.co.uk
Bartle Bogle Hegarty	www.bbh.co.uk
BMP DDB	www.bmp.co.uk
Cordiant	www.ccgww.com
DMBB	www.dmbb.com
Grey	www.grey.co.uk
J Walter Thompson	www.jwtworld.com
Leo Burnett	www.leoburnett.com
Lowe Lintas	www.lowehoward-spink.co.uk
McCann Erickson	www.mccann.com
Saatchi & Saatchi	www.saatchi-saatchi.com
Young & Rubicam	www.yandr.com

e-mail marketing

Alphasoft	www.alphasoftware.com
Arial Software	www.arialsoftware.com
Campaign	
Colorado Soft	www.coloradosoft.com
WorldMerge	

Direct Email List Source	www.copywriter.com/lists/
Direct Email Marketing	www.e-target.com
Direct Marketing Association	www.the-dma.com
Direct Marketing News	www.dmnews.com
ELetter	www.eletter.com
EverythingE-mail	www.everythingemail.com
infoUSA	www.infousa.com
InterACT	www.interact.com
MailKing	www.mailking.com
Mailing-Labels	www.mailing-labels.com
Stamps.com	www.stamps.com
Yahoo!	www.yahoo.com:companies:direct marketing:email maketing

banner advertising

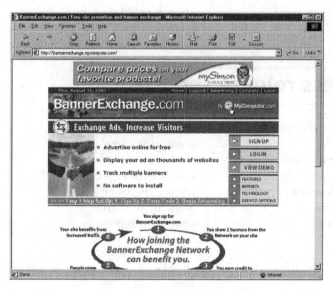

Figure 15.6 BannerExchange lets you swap banner ads – for free

Adbility.com	www.adbility.com
Adclub.net	www.adclub.net
Banneradnetwork.com	www.banneradnetwork.com
Bannerexchange.com	www.bannerexchange.com
Bannertips.com	www.bannertips.com
Bannerworkz.com	www.bannerworkz.com
Bcentral.com	www.bcentral.com
Budget Banners	www.budget-banners.com
Internet Link Exchange	www.bcentral.com
Outerplanet.com	www.outerplanet.com

online advertising agencies

DoubleClick	www.doubleclick.com
Ipro	www.ipro.com
Market Match	www.marketmatch,com
SoftBank Media	www.simweb.com
WebConnect	www.worlddata.com
WebTrack	www.webtrack.com

press release services

BusinessWire	www.businesswire.com
GINA	www.gina.com
Internet News Bureau	www.newsbureau.com
PRNewsTarget	www.newstarget.com
PRNewswire	www.prnewswire.com
URLwire	www.urlwire.com
Xpress Press	www.xpresspress.com

building websites

Your website is your all-day, everyday marketing event. It can be viewed just as easily by a potential customer in the next street as a customer in the next country. It enables you to advertise your range of products and services and promote your brand, without someone being present. With some careful planning, you can also provide automated features that supply answers to common questions from customers, product upgrades for existing customers, maps of local stockists, ways to make the most of your products and their glowing reviews.

By integrating an element of E-commerce, you can provide shopping features to automate the order-taking and payment process, provide areas for press and media information, and even support your reps with online sales kits. And lastly, you can provide stacks of resources and information that could be useful to a potential browser; if you sell coffee, include information on how it was grown and imported, how to make a perfect espresso or links to sites that sell mugs, biscuits and coffee-makers.

Before you create your killer website, you should look at the guides on design practice, programming and planning to help you turn your content into a usable and popular website. To help you design and produce the website, you will need to use specialist webpage editor software. And if you want to add a database or other advanced features such as a guestbook, discussion group or classified advertising, you will need to install and configure specialist software. Much of this specialist software is supplied on the Net through the big shareware libraries such as ScriptSearch and Freecode; you can search these sites for programs that you can often try out for free.

Once your website is finished, you will still need to promote it effectively to ensure that it is seen by potential visitors. One of the most important starting points is to make sure that your website details are correctly registered with all the major search engine sites (such as Yahoo, Excite and AltaVista). You could visit each in turn, but there are time-saving specialist websites such as SubmitIt that can send your site's details to dozens of search engines. Once you have done this basic groundwork, look at the section on marketing and advertising (page 111) for details of banner advertising schemes and e-mail marketing techniques that help attract visitors to your site.

advice for site builders

Builder.com	www.builder.com
Pages that suck	www.pagesthatsuck.com
WebDeveloper	www.webdeveloper.com
WebMonkey	www.webmonkey.com

webpage editors

Dreamweaver	www.macromedia.com
Fusion	www.netobjects.com
Frontpage	www.microsoft.com
HotDog	www.sausage.com
HoTMetaL	www.sq.com
PageMill	www.adobe.com
Visual Page	www.symantec.com

domain name registration

Network Solutions	www.networksolutions.com
NetNames	www.netnames.co.uk

QuickDomains   www.quickdomains.com
NetBenefit   www.netbenefit.com
NicNames   www.nicnames.co.uk
BudgetDomains   www.budgetdomains.net

Web databases

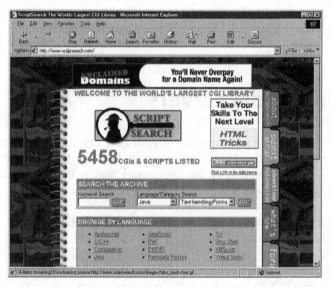

Figure 16.1 A low-cost route to adding a database is to use a free Perl script from ScriptSearch

Borland   www.borland.com
FileMaker Pro   www.filemaker.com
Freecode   www.freecode.com
Microrim   www.microrim.com
Microsoft   www.microsoft.com
Oracle   www.oracle.com
ScriptSearch   www.scriptsearch.com

website technical resources

ActiveX	www.microsoft.com
BrowserWatch	www.browserwatch.com
Clipart.com	www.clipart.com
Freecode	www.freecode.com
Java	www.java.com
JavaScript	www.javascript.com
Perl programming language	www.perl.org
ScriptSearch	www.scriptsearch.com
Shockwave	www.macromedia.com

multimedia servers

Want to do a live presentation of your new product range or chair an interactive video feedback session for key clients? Here are some of the main providers of the technology that will let you add this multimedia content to your website.

Media Server (Netscape)	http://home.netscape.com
NetShow (Microsoft)	www.microsoft.com
RealMedia	www.realaudio.com
StreamWorks (Xing)	www.xingtech.com
VDOLive (VDOnet)	www.vdo.com
WebTheater (VXtreme)	www.vxtreme.com

promoting websites

To ensure that your website appears in the results of each search engine query, you need to promote your site by registering it with each search engine. Either visit each of the major search engine sites or, to save time, use one of these online tools that can submit your site to all the search engines automatically.

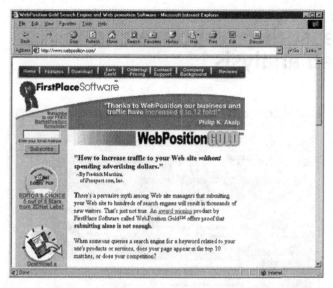

Figure 16.2 Check your website's ranking with the search engines using WebPosition

DidIt	www.did-it.com
Exploit	www.exploit.com
LinkPopularity	www.linkpopularity.com
SearchEngineWatch	www.searchenginewatch.com
Submit It	www.submit-it.com
WebPosition	www.webposition.com

what's new and award sites

Award sites listed	www.resoluteinc.com/cyberonline
Internet Magazine	www.Internet-magazine.com/bookmarks/
Netscape	www.netscape.com/netcenter/new.html
Yahoo!	www.yahoo.com/picks

measuring response and Web analysis

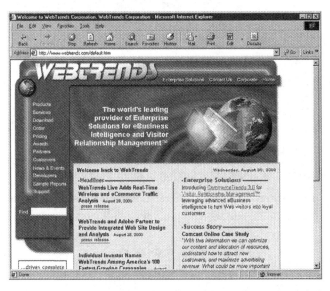

Figure 16.3 Use a visitor analysis product, like WebTrends, to help manage your site

Accrue Software	www.accrue.com
Analog	www.statslab.cam.ac.uk/~sret1/analog
Aptex	www.aptex.com
DoubleClick	www.doubleclick.com
GeoSys mapping	www.geosys.com
WebTrends	www.webtrends.com
Yahoo!	www.yahoo.com:Internet:web:analysis software

seventeen

E-commerce

Some websites are set up simply to provide a catalogue of products, but more and more companies are starting to realise the commercial potential of their sites by adding revenue-generating features. Some sites include an online shop, where customers can select and pay for products; other sites sell advertising space to generate money, while business-to-business sites can be set up to provide direct links between business partners. All three models use the Internet to provide an efficient, fast and relatively cost-effective way of taking orders and accepting payment for goods.

shopping carts

Actinic Catalog	www.actinic.com
Cart32	www.cart32.com
Cat@log 2.0	www.thevisionfactory.com
CheckOut! Pro	www.n2plus.com
COWS	www.cows.co.uk
Dansie Shopping Cart	www.dansie.net
EasyCart	www.easycart.com
FreeMerchant	www.freemerchant.com
IBM Net.Commerce	www.ibm.com/software/webservers/ commerce/
iCat	www.icat.com
InterShop	www.intershop.com
JShop Pro	www.jshop.co.uk
Mercantec SoftCart	www.mercantec.com

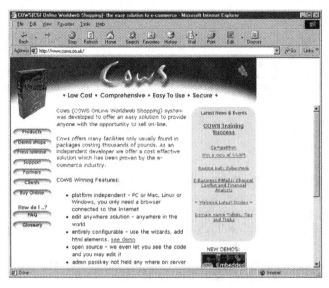

Figure 17.1 Cows provides a low-cost, effective Perl-based shopping cart

MiniVend	www.minivend.com
Miva Merchant	www.miva.com
PerlShop	www.arpanet.com
SalesCart	www.salescart.com
VIPCart	www.vipcart.com

turnkey shopping sites

addAshop	www.addashop.com
apoogee.com	www.apoogee.com
B2BXchange	www.b2bxchange.net
Betrindo Shop Builder	www.bg-net.com
Bigstep.com	www.bigstep.com
Clickandbuild	www.worldpay.com
Clickthings	www.clickthings.com
CNET Store.com	www.store.com
dibit.com	www.dibit.com

Figure 17.2 Click-n-Build is a turnkey shopping cart that works with the WorldPay credit-card processing site

EasyCart	www.easycart.com
E-Biz Builder	www.e-bizbuilder.com
eCongo	www.econgo.com
Ezystore	www.ezystore.com
FreeMerchant	www.freemerchant.com
Galaxy Mall	www.galaxymall.com
GeoShops	www.geocities.com/join/geoshops
goEmerchant.com	www.goemerchant.com
Goos.com	www.goos.com
iCat Corporation (2)	www.icat.com
InterTrade	www.itrade.net
JumboStore	www.jumbostore.com
Malldomain.com	www.malldomain.com
Max Computing Services	www.maxengine.com
Propel	www.propel.com
ShopBuilder	www.shopbuilder.com
ShopCreator	www.shopcreator.com
ShopSite	www.openmarket.com/shopsite
Stores Online	www.storesonline.com

Ubrandit.com	www.ubrandit.com
VirginBiz	www.virginbiz.net
Vstore	www.vstore.com
Yahoo! Store	http://store.yahoo.com

payment processing

If you want to accept credit-card payments online you will need to use a specialist company to manage the card authorisation and payment processing. In the UK there are a few specialists, in the US there are dozens. These companies all work invisibly, checking a customer's credit-card number, then managing the funds transfer from their card to your bank account. You usually need a special Internet merchant account to accept payments and you should check that your shopping cart software will work with the payment processing agency (not all are compatible with each other). Almost all agencies charge a fee or percentage of transactions – you can compare their rates with a tool like ShopForRates (www.shopforrates.com).

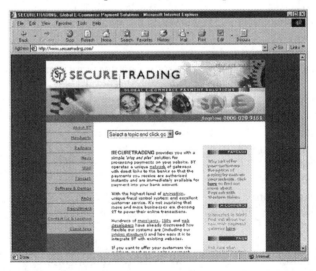

Figure 17.3 Secure Trading provide realtime credit-card processing for your shopping site

UK payment processing

Secure Trading	www.securetrading.com
Datacash	www.datacash.com
NetBanx	www.netbanx.co.uk
WorldPay	www.worldpay.com

US payment processing

1st American Card Service	www.1stamericancardservice.com
Advantage Merchant Services	www.creditcardprocessor.com
American Express	www.americanexpress.com/business
Authorize.Net	www.authorize.net
BankAmerica Merchant Services	www.bankamerica.com
Charge.Com	www.charge.com
Creditnet	www.creditnet.com
Electronic Payment Processing	www.eppinc.com
ePayments Resource Center	www.epaynews.com
GORealtime	www.gorealtime.com
iTransact	www.redicheck.com
Mastercard Merchant Site	www.mastercard.com/merchants
OpenMarket	www.openmarket.com
Pay2See.com	www.pay2see.com
Paylinx.com	www.paylinx.com

paying online

For the moment, credit cards are the accepted method of payment on the Net, but the future should see the take-up of new E-cash systems that are more convenient, secure and consumer-friendly (so you do not have to keep typing in your credit-card number). The latest developments include SET (secure electronic transaction), which offers a new standard that should make E-commerce wesbites easier to use. To make sure that your E-commerce site stays up to date, find out the latest developments on these sites.

digital cash

Figure 17.4   Find out about the future of cash at the National ECRC

DigiCash	www.digicash.com
National Electronic Commerce Resource Center	www.ecrc.ctc.com
Electronic Payment Mechanisms	www2.echo.lu/oii/en/payment.html
FAQ on digital cash	http://ganges.cs.tcd.ie/mepeirce/Project/Mlists/minifaq.html

Yahoo!   www.yahoo.com/
                                Business_and_Economy/
                                Electronic_Commerce/
                                Digital_Money/

SET

Secure Electronic Transaction   www.setco.org
SET FAQ   www.setco.org/faq.html
SET at Visa   www.visa.com
SET Sites   www.SET-Sites.com

consumer watchdogs

Setting up an online shop is a great way to offer far-flung consumers an efficient and cost-effective way to order your products. However, if you do not deliver on your promises or if you overcharge, supply poor-quality products or have no back-up or customer support, you will get complaints. The Internet empowers business, but it also empowers consumers to fight back and let any other potential customer know that your site is not worth a visit. Visit these consumer watchdog sites to see how to avoid the problems experienced on other sites.

Advertising Standards   www.asa.org.uk
   Association
Bad, Better and Best   www.webBbox.com
   Businesses Bulletin
   Board
Better Business Bureau   www.bbb.org
BizRate   www.bizrate.com
iLeveL   www.ilevel.com
Internet Advocacy Center   www.consumeradvocacy.com
Internet Consumer   www.isitsafe.com
   Assistance Bureau

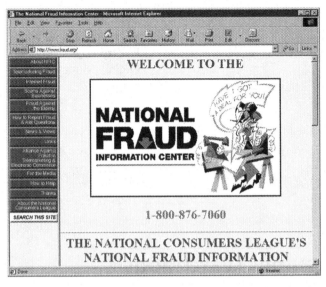

Figure 17.5 Rip off your customers and you will end up listed at Fraud.org

National Association of Citizens Advice Bureaux	www.nacab.org.uk
National Fraud Information Center	www.fraud.org
Office of Fair Trading	www.oft.gov.uk
Public Eye	www.thepubliceye.com/ review.htm
Trading Standards	www.tradingstandards.gov.uk
WebAssured	www.webassured.com

secure websites

One essential feature of any E-commerce site is a trusted, secure webpage, where customers can be confident that the personal information that they type in (such as a credit-card number) cannot be accessed by a hacker. The standard method of providing this security is called SSL – if you plan to setup an E-commerce site, you will need to understand what it does and how it works (in principal, if not the technical nitty-gritty). These sites will provide introductions to the subject.

Netscape's SSL Page	http://home.netscape.com/security/ techbriefs/ssl.html
SSL FAQ	www.consensus.com/security/ssl-talk-faq.html
Planet SSL	www.rsa.com/ssl/
Security and Encryption Links	www.cs.auckland.ac.nz/~pgut001/ links.html

digital signatures

Digital signatures are a way of proving that an e-mail message was really sent by you; it is a way of ensuring orders can only be

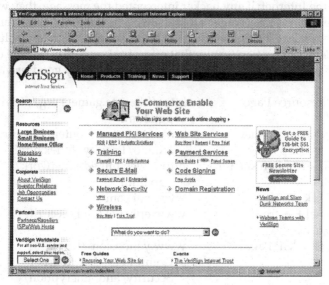

Figure 17.6 Protect the integrity of your e-mail with a digital signature from Verisign

authorised by one person and provides a secure method of confirming contractual details or official orders. Find out how to implement your own digital signature at these sites.

Tutorial of Digital signatures	www.abanet.org/scitech/ec/isc/dsg-tutorial.html
Digital Signature Legislation	http://cwis.kub.nl/~frw/people/hof/DS-lawsu.htm
EFF digital signature archive	www.eff.org/pub/Privacy/Digital_signature/
Legislative matrix for digital signature	www.magnet.state.ma.us/itd/legal/matrix10.htm
Verisign	www.verisign.com

encryption

When you send an e-mail message, the words are sent as plain text over the Internet; if any hacker intercepted the message, they would be able to read it. To get around this, you can encrypt (scramble) your message before sending it. Most e-mail programs include a low-level encryption feature that offers basic security, but one of the most popular, high-security systems is PGP (pretty good privacy).

PGP Resource Page	http://thegate.gamers.org/~tony/pgp.html
Protect your privacy	www.cnet.com/Content/Features/Howto/Privacy/index.html
MIT distribution site for PGP	http://web.mit.edu/network/pgp.html
Network Associates	www.nai.com
Personal Electronic Security	www.epix.net/~alf/Security/
Yahoo! – PGP Page	www.yahoo.com/text/Computers_and_Internet/Security_and_Encryption/PGP___Pretty_Good_Privacy/

stocks and shares

The Web provides a wealth of information about publicly traded companies. You can use the Web to check your competitor's stock price (or your own), look at a general composite index minute by minute or monitor how a sector, such as telecoms, is doing in a particular country.

Many business people own shares on a personal level, so this section would be of interest to help monitor their portfolio. However, the amount of information and informed commentary on shares and market conditions provides a great research tool if you are trying to find out about a company, sector or country.

You can check the share price of a particular company at any time, for free, using sites such as iii, or you can add a ticker-line to your computer's desktop display to see realtime prices of shares as they are traded. To help you analyse price movements, there are specialist charting sites that track the ups and downs and help predict future prices. Finally, you can look for expert commentary from well-known market gurus – either written or in mini video presentations online.

share portals

Bloomberg   www.bloomberg.com
FinanceWise   www.financewise.com
Global Investor   www.global-investor.com

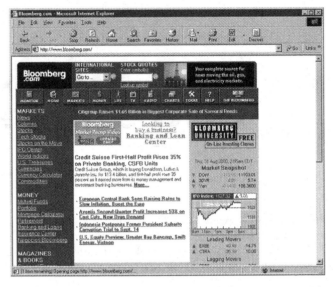

Figure 18.1 Bloomberg provides a vast, central share resource with prices, reports and analysis

iii (interactive investor international)	www.iii.co.uk
imoney	www.imoney.com
InvestorGuide	www.investorguide.com
MoneyeXtra	www.moneyextra.co.uk
The DataChimp	www.datachimp.com
Zacks.com	www.zacks.com

market data and prices

Almost all the major portals provide stock market prices – and let you set up a portfolio of shares to monitor. Most data sites also include extra features to display historical charts of price movements and analysis of trends.

1010 WallStreet	www.1010wallstreet.com
AltaVista	www.altavista.com

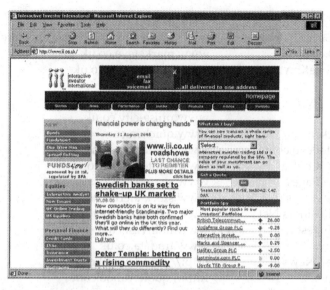

Figure 18.2 iii provides share and unit trust prices from stock exchanges across the world

Barchart.com	www.barchart.com
BigCharts	www.bigcharts.com
Bloomberg	www.bloomberg.co.uk
Bridge	www.bridge.com
Bullsession.com	www.bullsession.com
Charting UK Share	http://metronet.co.uk/bigwood/shares/
Citifeed	www.citifeed.co.uk
Digital Look	www.digitallook.com
Equity Index Trends	www.equityindextrends.com
European Investor	www.europeaninvestor.com
Excite!	www.excite.co.uk
Free RealTime	www.freerealtime.com
FreeQuotes	www.freequotes.co.uk
Fund-info.com	www.fund-info.com
Futures Pager	www.futurespager.com
Hemmington Scott	www.hemscott.com
Hoovers Online	www.hoovers.com
iii (interactive investor international)	www.iii.co.uk

Index Direct	www.indexdirect.co.uk
InfoBeat Finance	www.infobeat.com/cb/cgi/cb_merc.cgi
Market-Eye	www.marketeye.co.uk
MoneyeXtra	www.moneyextra.co.uk
MSN	www.msn.co.uk
NASDAQ	www.nasdaq.co.uk
Pulse	www.pulse-city.co.uk
Quicken	www.quicken.com
QuoteBeep.com	www.quotebeep.com
QuoteCentral	www.quotecentral.com
Share Pages	www.sharepages.com
Stock Alerts	www.stock-alerts.com
UK Business Net	www.ukbusinessnet.com
UK Invest	www.ukinvest.com
Updata	www.updata.co.uk
Wired News	http://stocks.wired.com
Yahoo!	http://quote.yahoo.com

realtime share prices

Most market data sites delay the share price information by 10–20 minutes (data is cheaper when it is old). But you can get free real-time share prices from a few sites – you will see the prices move as the shares are traded.

Bridge	www.bridge.com
Bullsession	www.bullsession.com
Citifeed	www.citifeed.co.uk
Free RealTime	www.freerealtime.com
FreeQuotes	www.freequotes.co.uk
Market-Eye	www.marketeye.co.uk
QuoteCentral	www.quotecentral.com

stock exchanges

World Stock Exchanges	www.hougie.co.uk/ exchange.htm
Australian Stock Exchange	www.asx.com.au
Boston Stock Exchange	www.bostonstock.com
Chicago Stock Exchange	www.chicagostockex.com
Deutsche Börse	www.exchange.de
NASDAQ-Amex	www.nasdaq.com
London Stock Exchange	www.londonstock exchange.com
techMARK	www.londonstock exchange.com/ techmark
AIM	www.londonstock exchange.com/aim
New York Stock Exchange	www.nyse.com
New Zealand Stock Exchange	www.nzse.co.nz
Hong Kong Stock Exchange	www.sehk.com.hk
Paris Stock Exchange	www.bourse-de-paris.fr
Tokyo Stock Exchange	www.tse.or.jp
Toronto Stock Exchange	www.tse.com

specialist investments

Coffee, Sugar and Cocoa Exchange	www.csce.com
Currency Trends	www.updatenews.com
Diamond Stocks	www.diamondstocks.com
Gold Eagle	www.gold-eagle.com
Oanda	www.oanda.com
Oil-n-Gas	www.oil-n-gas.com

futures and options

Derivatives Strategy	www.derivatives.com
Deutsche Terminborse	www.dtb.de
Futures and Options World	www.fow.com
Futures Magazine Online	www.futuresmag.com
Futures.Net	www.futures.net
INO Global Markets	www.ino.com
LIFFE	www.liffe.com
Matif	www.matif.fr
National Futures Association	www.nfa.futures.org
Options Industry Council	www.optionscentral.com

online brokers

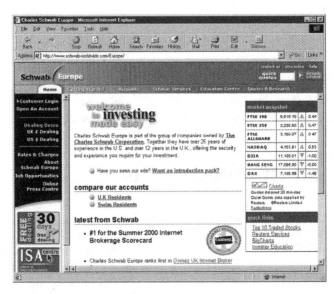

Figure 18.3 Deal online with Charles Schwab, one of the biggest Web-based brokers

City ShareShop	www.cityshareshop.co.uk
Barclays Stockbrokers	www.barclays-stockbrokers.co.uk
Branston and Gothard	www.branstonandgothard.com
Cannon Trading Co.	www.commoditiestrading.com
Charles Schwab Europe	www.schwab-worldwide.com
Charles Stanley & Co.	www.charles-stanley.co.uk
Datek	www.datek.com
Discount Brokers: On The Net	http://advocacy-net.com/discbmks.htm
DLJ Direct	www.dljdirect.co.uk
Gómez Directory of Brokers	www.gomez.com
Internet Investing	www.internetinvesting.com
Keynote Web Brokerage Index	www.keynote.com/measures/brokers/
Killik & Co	www.killik.co.uk
Lebenthal & Co.	www.lebenthal.com
Maddison.com	www.maddison.com
Money.com	www.pathfinder.com/money/broker/
myBROKER	www.mybroker.co.uk
Mydiscountbroker.com	www.mydiscountbroker.com
Navillus Securities	www.navillus.com
Options Direct	www.options-direct.co.uk
The Share Centre	www.share.co.uk
Stocktrade	www.stocktrade.co.uk

new issues/IPOs

Direct IPO	www.directipo.com
Direct Stock Market	www.dsm.com
epo.com	www.epo.com
IPO Central	www.ipocentral.com
IPO.com	www.ipo.com
IPO Data Systems	www.ipodata.com
IPO Maven	www.ipomaven.com
Wit Capital	www.witcapital.com

Figure 18.4   Track new issues with specialist site, epo.com

travel

The Web is working hard to try and oust traditional travel agents; it promises low-price tickets, instant confirmation, panoramic views of a hotel, cheap insurance, custom itinaries, maps, guides and opinions – and all in your own time, at your own pace.

The travel sites on the Web divide into various sectors. Some, such as eBookers are purely commercial and offer an efficient and effective way to source cut-price hotels, plane and train tickets. Others include guides and reviews of resorts to give a cross between a travel brochure and a travel guide-book. Lastly, there are information-only sites, such as Lonely Planet, that provide advice, guides and opinions from other travellers.

Most of the online travel agents cater to individual travellers going on holiday. A few can handle complex itinaries from business travellers, with the exception of BizTravel. However, all the travel agents offer business-class travel options – often at vastly reduced rates – or you can use one of the business jet charter services, if you and colleagues want to fly in style.

Many professional business travellers already have their own requirements – particular seat, preferred flight time and frequent flier scheme. You can use a site such as BizTravel to help track your frequent flier points (across several schemes) – it can even ensure that when you next make your travel plans your points are maximised.

business travel guides

Fit for Business   www.fitforbusiness.com
Oanda Currency Conversion www.oanda.com

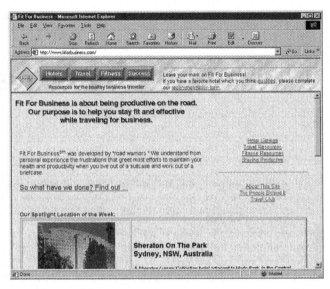

Figure 19.1 Get a hotel with a gym – guides for sporty travellers at Fit for Business

The EmbassyWeb	www.embpage.org
How Far Is It?	www.indo.com/distance/
Placeware	www.placeware.com
Roadnews.com	www.roadnews.com

guides and maps

CIA Worldbook	www.odci.gov/cia/ publications/factbook/
City Net	www.city.net
Lonely Planet	www.lonelyplanet.co.uk
MapQuest	www.mapquest.com
Maps Worldwide	www.mapsworldwide.co.uk
MultiMap	www.multimap.com
The Original Tipping Page	www.tipping.org
Railtrack	www.railtrack.co.uk

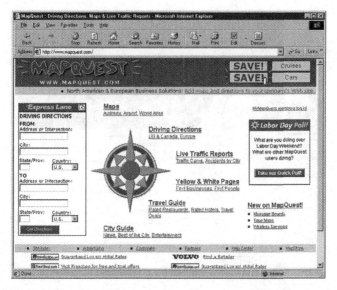

Figure 19.2   Check a map of almost any city with MapQuest

Rough Guides	www.roughguides.com
Travelang	www.travlang.com
Travel Etiquette	www.traveletiquette.com
UK Street Map	www.streetmap.co.uk

airlines

Every major airline has its own website; most provide timetables, display seating patterns and usually let you book online or check on your current frequent-flyer points total. For a list of all the airlines, visit a directory such as Airlines of the World (www.flyaow.com); you will find the official airline site great for checking times, but prices are often cheaper at dedicated online travel agents (see later in this section).

Aer Lingus	www.aerlingus.ie
Aeroflot	www.aeroflot.org

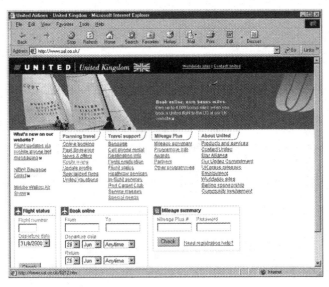

Figure 19.3 UAL, like most airlines, provides timetables, special offers and online booking

Air Canada	www.aircanada.ca
Air France	www.airfrance.com
Alitalia	www.italiatour.com
American	www.americanair.com
British Airways	www.british-airways.com
British Midland	www.iflybritishmidland.com
Cathay Pacific	www.cathaypacific.com
Continental	www.flycontinental.com
Delta	www.delta-air.com
EasyJet	www.easyjet.co.uk
El Al	www.elal.co.il
Go	www.go-fly.com
Iberia	www.iberia.com
KLM	www.klmuk.com
Lufthansa	www.lufthansa.co.uk
Olympic	www.olympic-airways.gr
Qantas	www.qantas.com
Ryanair	www.ryanair.ie
SAS	www.sas.se

Singapore Airlines	www.singaporeair.com
TWA	www.twa.com
United	www.ual.co.uk
Varig	www.varig.com.br
Virgin	www.fly.virgin.com

airports

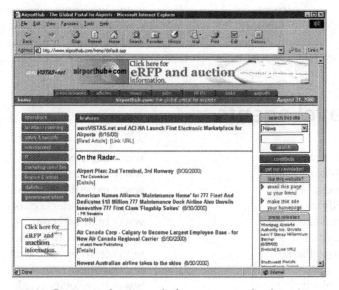

Figure 19.4 Get your bearings before you reach the airport, with AirportHub

BAA	www.baa.co.uk
Gatwick Airport	www.gatwickairport.co.uk
Glasgow Airport	www.baa.co.uk/glasgow
Heathrow Airport	www.baa.co.uk/heathrow
Stansted Airport	www.stansted.co.uk
British International Airports	www.bia.co.uk
Jane's Airport Review	http://jar.janes.com
AIRbase One	www.airbase1.com

Airlines Online	www.4airlines.com
AirNav	www.airnav.com
Airport CheckIn	www.airport.checkin.com
AirportHub	www.airporthub.com
AirportsAmerica.com	www.airportsamerica.com
Ankunft.com	www.ankunft.com
EuroTerminal Airport	www.euroterminal.com
French Airports	www.french-airports.com
QuickAID Information Directory	www.quickaid.com
Birmingham International Airport	www.bhx.co.uk
Liverpool Airport	www.livairport.com
London City Airport	www.londoncityairport.com
London Luton Airport	www.london-luton.com
Manchester Airport	www.manairport.co.uk

travel agents

A2bTravel	www.a2btravel.com
eBookers	www.ebookers.com
Expedia	www.expedia.co.uk
Trailfinders	www.trailfinders.co.uk
Biztravel.com	www.biztravel.com
HotelWorld	www.hotelworld.com
Leisure Planet	www.leisureplanet.com
Eurostar	www.eurostar.com
Travelocity	www.travelocity.co.uk

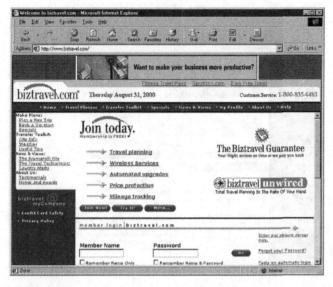

Figure 19.5   Of the hundreds of online travel agents, few deal exclusively with business travellers, except BizTravel

personal jets

NetJets	www.netjets.com
FlexJet	www.flexjet.com
Lear Jet	www.learjet.com

hotels

1–2-3 Go Travel	www.123-go.org
2Stay.com	www.2stay.com
A-thru-Z HotelFinder	www.from-a-z.com
AA Guide	www.theaa.co.uk
Accommodation Search	www.ase.net
Best Hotel	www.best-hotel.com

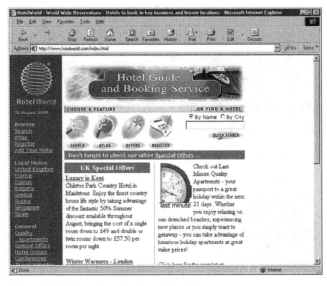

Figure 19.6   Find a hotel with HotelWorld

British Hotel Reservation	www.bhrc.co.uk
Holiday Rentals	www.holiday-rentals.co.uk/
Hotel Book	www.hotelbook.com
Hotel File	www.hotelfile.co.uk
Hotel Net	www.hotelnet.co.uk
HotelWorld	www.hotelworld.com
Infotel	www.infotel.co.uk
Leisure Planet	www.leisureplanet.com/
Small Luxury Hotels	www.slh.com

frequent flier schemes

AirBank	www.airawards.com
FrequentFlier	www.frequentflier.com
WebFlyer	www.webflyer.com

discussing business

One of the most popular ways to use the Net is to discuss things: business ideas, solving problems, new marketing strategies, prices, staff, contacts, complaints, tips, or just worries. The Net is very good at bringing together large, dispersed, groups of users who can meet in one place and discuss just about anything. There are three basic types of meeting place on the Net where you can meet up and chat: discussion groups, mailing lists and newsgroups.

For marketing and business discussions, you will probably find that the discussion groups that form part of marketing or business magazines and advice websites prove the most useful, but it is well worth touring the mailing lists and newsgroups to see what is going on.

One of the most popular features of many business and specialist marketing websites are their discussion groups. Almost all the websites produced by the major business magazines – such as Inc. and Fast Company – include a discussion group.

Mailing lists are a great way to distribute messages to a group of people with the same interests. It is a perfect way to keep up to date with a particular subject, special-interest group or colleagues. Unlike Web-based discussion groups, mailing lists work through your normal e-mail program. The group is simply a collection of e-mail addresses of subscribers, managed automatically by a special program, normally called a list server.

The last forum are newsgroups (sometimes called Usenet); these offer a vast range of very active discussion forums where just about anything goes. They work just like an office notice board – anyone can post a message that can then be read by anyone else. You might not like everything that is said in them, but it is a great place to get feedback, opinions and research.

finding mailing lists

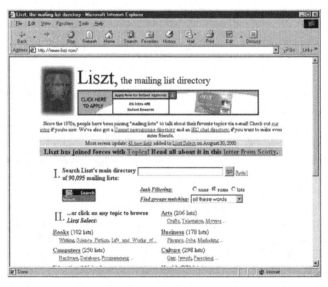

Figure 20.1   Find a mailing list with Liszt

CataList	www.lsoft.com/lists/listref.html
Liszt	www.liszt.com
Tile.net	www.tile.net
eGroups	www.egroups.com

discussion groups and chat forums

Most big business websites (especially business magazine sites) have active discussion groups (see page 103) or use a specialist search engine such as Talkway (www.talkway.com) or ForumOne (www.forumone.com) to find your site. Alternatively, try these groups.

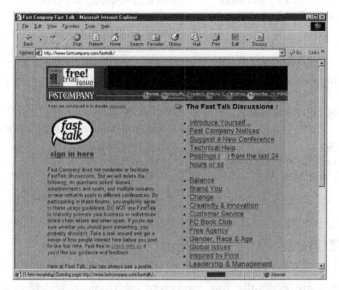

Figure 20.2   Chat online at Fast Company's discussion group

About.com	http://entrepreneurs.about.com
Association for International Business	www.profunda.dk/resources/ business/aib.html
Business Credit Talk	www.igotit.com
Business 2.0	www.business2.com
BusinessWeek	www.businessweek.com
Excite Chat	www.excite.com
Fast Company	www.fastcompany.com
Financial Times	www.ft.com
Fortune Magazine	www.fortune.com
Guru.com	www.guru.com
Harvard Business School ListServs	www.hbsp.harvard.edu/listservs/ index.html
International Trade	www.intl-trade.com/wwwboard/
LinkExchange	www.linkexchange.com

mail-list.com	www.mail-list.com
Nvst.com Funding Forum	www.nvst.com
Optima Trade Board	www.trade-board.com
Publicity and Promotion Discussion Board	www.free-publicity.com
Red Herring	www.redherring.com
Sage	www.sagesoft.co.uk/accounts/
SOHO Discussion Group	www.zdnet.com/cc/chat.html
Startup Network	www.delphi.com/ startupnetwork/start/
Yahoo! Business Finance	http://messages.yahoo.com/ yahoo/business_and_finance/
Wired	www.wired.com
Women Entrepreneurs Online Network	www.weon.com

E-zines

E-zines are generally fun, irreverent electronic newsletters about sports, music, hobbies and life – but some do cover business – admittedly, usually with an alternative angle. Finding an E-zine is usually the most difficult part of the job; here are just about the only specialist search engines:

eZine Center	www.ezinecenter.com
HotWired	www.hotwired.com/zines/

finding newsgroups

Newsgroups are a separate part of the Internet to the Web and normally need special newsgroup reader software (that is often part of your e-mail software) to read or post messages. However, the Web and newsgroup environments meet on specialist search engine

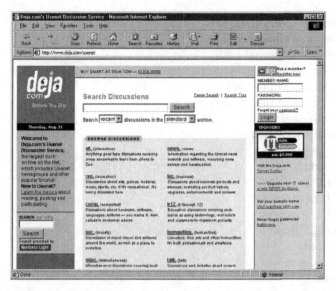

Figure 20.3 Find a newsgroup or search newsgroup postings with Deja

sites that let you hunt through archives of past messages to find a newsgroup that interests you.

Deja	www.deja.com
Newsgroup Directory	www.tile.net/news
Remarq	www.remarq.com
Usenet Info Center	http://metalab.unc.edu/usenet-i/

business newsgroups

alt.make.money.fast
alt.biz.marketplace.international
alt.business
alt.business.accountability
alt.business.career-opportunities.executives
alt.business.franchise
alt.business.hospitality

alt.business.import-export
alt.business.insurance
alt.business.internal-audit
alt.business.misc
alt.business.multi-level
alt.business.multi-level.scam.scam.scam
alt.business.seminars
biz.comp.accounting
biz.entrepreneurs
biz.marketplace
clari.biz.briefs
clari.biz.currencies
clari.biz.economy
clari.biz.industry
misc.taxes
misc.taxes.moderated
sci.econ

free e-mail accounts

If you post messages (contribute) to newsgroups on a regular basis, you will need to supply an e-mail address to identify your messages. If you provide your main work e-mail address, you will soon find that your inbox is overflowing with junk spam messages – unscrupulous marketeers scan newsgroups and automatically pull off e-mail addresses of contributors, then resell these as valid lists. The way around this is to register for a free e-mail account that is separate from your main account. Many of the main search engines and portals offer free e-mail accounts – here are some of the best known.

Bigfoot	www.bigfoot.com
Cometmail	www.cometmail.com
Excite!	www.excite.com
Hotmail	www.hotmail.com

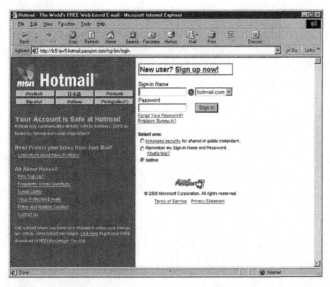

Figure 20.4 Hotmail is one of the most popular free e-mail services – essential if you are planning to use newsgroups

RocketMail   www.rocketmail.com
Yahoo!   www.yahoo.com

getting online

Before you can start using the Internet, you have got to get connected and get online. This section is a basic guide to getting your computer – or your office network – online. If you are already online, you can ignore this section and simply use the rest of the book to improve your marketing strategy online.

For most users and companies, the gateway to the Internet is through a specialist communications company, called an Internet service provider (ISP). The ISP provides a telephone access number for your modem, ISDN or ADSL connection, together with a user name and password. Once you have installed the software you need to connect and use the Internet, you will need to configure it to call the ISP's access number and make the connection.

Once you are online, you can browse the Web, send and receive electronic mail and publish your own website. If it all sounds rather complex, do not worry. Thankfully, almost all new computers now come with all the extra software you need pre-installed, and ISPs generally send out custom CD-ROMs with automated installation guides, ensuring you get online with just a few clicks.

In order to access the Internet, you need to choose an Internet service provider (ISP). If you want to publish your own website, you will need a company that can host your site and let you use your own domain name and advanced features such as adding a database.

choosing an ISP

You need to set up an account with an ISP to provide your path to the Internet. It works as a middleman, providing a local telephone number to dial in to and connect to its main computers, which form part of the Internet. Only the very biggest sites or corporations link directly to the Internet; everyone else makes use of an ISP and leaves them to manage the complex network connections.

Essentially there are just two types of ISP: one charges a fee and the other is free. Free ISPs are tempting, but are geared to home users and often do not support the extra features you will need to build a business website. Some ISPs now even provide free telephone calls to subscribers, particularly in the evening or weekends. A couple of companies – AOL and CompuServe – offer global access numbers that are a boon if you or your colleagues travel on business and want to stay in touch. However, for most companies you simply want a fast, reliable and low-cost connection to the Internet. One of the best ways to choose an ISP is to use the league tables produced by the online Internet magazines that rank different ISPs by speed and features. Visit .Net (www.netmag.co.uk) or Internet Magazine (www.emap.co.uk) or Internet Works (www.iwks.co.uk).

An ISP provides the connection and route to the Internet, but you do not have to use it for all your Net jobs. There are lots of Web-hosting companies that specialise in providing Web space on which to store your website pages; you will still need an ISP to get online, but the Web-hosting company might be able to provide a better deal than the ISP for your Web space requirements – simply because they do not have the overhead of managing telephone connections for users' modems.

getting on the Internet

You can connect just about any computer to the Internet – from a high-powered workstation to a pocket organiser. You do not even need a computer to get the benefits of the Net. If you have a mobile phone or pager, you can use this to receive information from some websites. And if your office has a network installed, you can link everyone on the network to the Internet very easily, but you will probably need extra hardware and software.

If you are connecting just one computer, the easiest way is to use a modem and a normal phone line. If you plan to make a lot of use of the Net, or if you are connecting the entire office, you will soon get complaints about slow speed from the users and you should install a faster link such as ISDN or ADSL (asymmetric digital subscriber line). In the UK, there is a small, business-friendly version of ISDN called Business Highway, but with the arrival of ADSL, this has been dealt a death-blow.

ISDN provides a relatively fast connection, but the latest technology is ADSL, which is proving hard to beat. You can get a permanent connection to the Internet for a fixed monthly subscription of around £50. It is many times faster than ISDN and can be a lot cheaper in call charges, making it an ideal route for offices and high-traffic users. If you do sign up for ADSL, make sure that you also install some form of firewall – it is far more susceptible to attack than standard dial-up connections such as ISDN.

To share your high-speed link across all the computers in the office, you will need to install a special device called a router. This connects the office network to your ISDN or ADSL line and automatically manages the connection to the Net anytime someone on the local office network starts a web browser or e-mail application. A specialist business ISP will be able to supply all the equipment you require – pre-configured – to connect everyone on your network to the Net.

why it is always so slow

The Internet sometimes seems to grind to a standstill, but, just as unexpectedly, it can zing along at a cracking rate. The performance you see has a little to do with your computer, more to do with the type of connection, and far more related to the traffic jams elsewhere in the world on the Net.

The speed of your connection (modem, ISDN or ADSL link) determines how fast you can transfer information to and from your computer, but you are still just as likely to hit congestion on the backbone (the main motorway of data flow that links your ISP to all the other providers). As more users log in at peak time, the motorway chokes up – so best to avoid early evening or your local time equivalent to when the US wakes up.

office net policy

Connect everyone in your office to the Net and there is the chance that they will all suddenly start playing online games, ordering their shopping, spending hours in chat rooms or viewing pornography. The Internet is supposed to improve productivity, but instead you might suddenly find productivity collapses – unless you provide a firm office policy and install a way of policing it.

If you connect your office network to the Internet, there are two new problems you will have to deal with:

- colleagues accessing inappropriate sites to view smut or wasting time playing games
- misusing the channel to send unsuitable, unwanted or libellous e-mail messages.

The first problem is relatively simple to manage and depends a lot on your office policy. If you do not mind employees booking their holidays online, ordering their shopping or visiting pornography sites, then there is nothing to worry about. However, it would be sensible to draw up a list of things you would rather the employees did not do. Make sure everyone knows this and respects it. If you want to prevent any infringement to these rules, you could install management software to shut down a user's session on the Net as soon as they try and access a forbidden site, and send a warning message to a supervisor.

The second problem is far more difficult to solve – let alone define for your office policy. It covers your colleagues sending information over the Net, particularly by e-mail. E-mail, as a writing medium, encourages sloppy writing, gossip, and far worse. In the US, recent court cases have found companies liable if an employee sends un-wanted, libellous or sexually provocative e-mail messages – even if meant as a joke.

Email is also particularly good for quick personal messages, party planning, or even job applications. However, it is hard to set down even basic rules covering use of e-mails, let alone how they should be written. Some big companies now install message scanning utilities (see the Directory, page 174), which run on the office network server and look for key words in any e-mail messages. If a message contains words such as *sex*, *secret* or even *job application*, the entire message can be stopped before it gets to the recipient.

setting up the software

To use the Internet, you need to install and configure special software on your computer to manage the connection and to let you view Web pages and read e-mail. However, all the software is normally pre-installed on new computers, and most ISPs will also send you a CD-ROM with similar pre-configured software ready to install. If you have a CD-ROM from your ISP, insert it in the drive and follow the instructions. Both Windows 98 and 2000 as well as Macintosh System 8 include an automated installation process that leads you through a set of simple, step-by-step procedures to configure the pre-installed software. Follow either process and you will end up with all the software you need, ready to connect to the Net.

Once you sign up with an ISP you will receive a user name, a password, an e-mail address and the telephone access number you use to connect and get online. If you register with AOL, CompuServe or an ISP that supplies a complete installation kit, simply insert the CD-ROM they send you and follow the simple instructions – the software automatically generates a user name and supplies the access phone number ready for your computer to dial.

As well as these basic bits of information, you will be sent a list of settings that you will need in order to send and receive e-mail messages and access newsgroups. The Microsoft Windows or Macintosh System 8 Internet installers both guide you through the process of typing these settings into the correct section of the software. Again, if you have subscribed to AOL, CompuServe or an ISP that provides a complete automated installation package, these settings will be filled in automatically.

To start using the Web, double-click on the Web browser icon on your desktop (or the AOL or CompuServe icon, if you have signed up with these providers) and the software will start. It automatically dials the telephone access number, supplies your user name and password, and sets up your connection to the Net.

When you are connected to the Net, Windows will display a tiny icon in the bottom right-hand corner of the screen with two green squares linked. If you see this, you are online. The squares should flash bright green to show information is being transferred. The top square is the distant computer at the ISP and the bottom square represents your computer. If you are connecting through a network, you will not see this icon.

Once you are connected, your browser automatically displays a nominated Web page, called its *home page* (normally your ISP's main page). You can change this easily so that you see your favourite financial page, newspaper or even the latest prices for your portfolio of shares by selecting the Tools/Internet Options menu in IE (Internet Explorer) or Edit/Preferences in Navigator and click on the button USE CURRENT PAGE to automatically insert the current site address. Next time you start the browser, it will display your favourite Web page.

browsing the Web

To visit a website, you have to type in the website's full address (called its URL) in the address box that is just under the menu bar in the top left-hand corner of your web browser. It is probably already displaying the address of the current home page. Just type over this – for example *www.wilsonweb.com* for the excellent marketing portal, WilsonWeb. You do not need to type in the initial bit of an address – the browser fills this in for you. Press RETURN and your browser tries to find and display the page. If it cannot find the site or page, you will see an error message; check you have typed the address in correctly and try again.

The main area of the Web browser displays the Web page. Hyperlinks are normally displayed as blue underlined text. As you move your pointer over a link you will see it change to a pointing finger icon. Click and you will jump to a new page. You can display several separate copies of the browser window by pressing CTRL-N (or APPLE-N on a Mac). Each window works independently, so you can view separate sites or pages in each.

electronic mail

It is no exaggeration to say that electronic mail will totally transform your communications. You can receive marketing tips, newsletters, or news headlines through e-mail – or keep in touch with your colleagues, customers and professional contacts. To send or receive electronic mail messages you need an e-mail program – and an Internet connection to send off the messages. If you have a relatively new computer, it already has e-mail software pre-installed as part of the Web browser software supplied by Microsoft or Netscape.

If you are on an office network, you should check with your IT manager which is the preferred software for your installation. Alternatively, if your ISP has sent you a CD-ROM with pre-configured software, you can use this instead. If you are configuring the software pre-installed on your computer (that is, not pre-configured and supplied by your ISP), then make sure that you have your e-mail address, user name, password and the address of the computer that manages e-mail at the ISP (usually two names called, for example, *smtp.demon.co.uk* and *pop.demon.co.uk*).

Do not forget that e-mail is sent as plain text – if anyone intercepts the message, they can read it. To prevent this, protect sensitive e-mails by encrypting the contents. Use the built-in feature in your e-mail program or for ultimate security, use the PGP (pretty good privacy) system (www.pgp.com).

e-mail standards

Most e-mail users work with one of the standard Internet e-mail systems, normally provided by their ISP. When you sign up, you configure your computer to send and receive mail messages through the ISP's central mail server computer. This computer temporarily stores any incoming mail till you go online and download the messages to your computer. If you send a message, your e-mail software transfers it to the server, which in turn sends it over the Internet to its destination.

business-to-business bible _____

E-mail is normally sent using a system called SMTP (simple mail transfer protocol) and received using a different system called POP3 (post office protocol-3). Almost all e-mail programs support this SMTP/POP3 mix of standards. Most decent ISPs will provide pre-configured software in their starter packs. If not, you will be sent the addresses of the ISP's mail server (normally one for incoming, one for outgoing mail). A new, more flexible e-mail standard is slowly growing in popularity. Called IMAP (internet message access protocol), it lets you read your mail, even if you are away from your computer. Almost all the latest e-mail software programs support this new standard, but unless you work in a big company, it is unlikely that you will use this feature immediately.

Web-based e-mail

So far, we have covered e-mail that you send and receive with a special program running on your computer. It is fast, flexible and still the most popular way of managing mail messages. However, there is an alternative way of managing you e-mail, using a program that runs on a remote website and is accessed through a Web page, displayed in your standard Web browser. You can send and receive standard mail messages, have your own address, but have the advantage of accessing your messages from anywhere in the world that has access to the Web – an Internet café, library or workplace.

Perhaps the best feature is that you can get a Web-based e-mail account for free from hundreds of different suppliers (such as Yahoo, Excite, and CometMail – see the Directory, page 173). Users that do not have a computer at home often set up a Web-based e-mail address, and it is also a good way to create a personal e-mail address that does not clog up your office account.

addressing e-mail

If you send a message to an e-mail address that does not exist, the message will come straight back again; this is called a bounce and tells you within minutes that the message could not be delivered. In most cases, the returned message will also contain extra information that tells you what went wrong – the user name might not be recognised by the server or perhaps the server is not responding at that moment.

Unfortunately, there is no complete, central directory of e-mail addresses to help you find someone's address. You have got three options: phone them and ask them, visit their company's Web site to see if there is a contact list or search one of the small directories of addresses that do exist (such as Four11 at www.four11.com).

Almost every e-mail program lets you send messages to more than one person at a time. This is great if you want to set up a newsletter with a small circulation or simply keep colleagues in the loop about a project. There are three address panels in your e-mail program where you can enter a recipient's address:

To: will send the message to the address of the person in this panel. You can list several addresses (separated by a comma or semicolon or space), in which case each person gets their own individual message and does not realise it has been sent to anyone else.

CC: (short for carbon copy) works with the *To:* field. Type in the address of another person who should see a copy of this message. The person in the *To:* field will be told who else has seen the message.

BCC: (short for blind carbon copy) works with the *To:* field (and the *CC:* field, if you want). If you type in an address here, they will receive a copy of the message, but the person in the *To:* field will not know that a copy has been sent.

The basic addressing features of your e-mail software are fine if you want to set up a small-circulation newsletter with fewer than a hundred names. Any more than this and you will find it easier to use a special mailing list program. Some contact managers, such as ACT!, Maximizer or GoldMine have e-mail-merge facilities and can handle several hundred e-mail messages per session.

The problem with both of these systems is that you are doing the work of sending a message from your desktop computer. A far more efficient way is to use special software that runs on your server computer (or your ISP's server). This has a faster link to the Net and provides a more efficient solution. You submit a list of recipients and a text file to be sent to each, and the soft-ware pumps out the messages. Visit EverythingE-mail (www. everythingemail.com) for links to dozens of mass-mailing programs.

sending to fax, pager or telephone

Your e-mail messages do not have to go to another computer. You can send messages to a normal fax machine, a pager or a mobile phone (with or without WAP (wireless application protocol)).

If you are travelling and only have an e-mail connection, but need to send a message to a colleague who only has a fax machine, use an e-mail-fax gateway that links the two systems. Some are free, others will charge you. The free systems tend to include a line of advertis-ing at the bottom of each fax, but are fast and efficient. Have a look at the efficient TPC (www.tpc.int), the gaudy Zipfax site (www. zipfax.com) or the simple Oxford University site (info.ox.ac.uk/ fax/).

Although the main mobile phone providers let you send text mes-sages between phones, it is a different matter when it is Web-to-phone. They are all trial systems, but at the time of going to press, only Orange (www.orange.co.uk) seems to provide a consistent service, with Vodafone (www.vodafone.co.uk) promising to offer the service soon.

security and viruses

Scare stories in newspapers ensure that most companies know about the security risks of the Internet – but not all treat it as a priority. The reality is that the risks are low, but you should still take sensible precautions to protect your company's computers and local area network (LAN).

If you plan to link just one computer to the Net, the risks are minimal. However, most companies link their LAN to the Internet and share access among users in the company. Once you connect your network to the Internet, you leave your company's computers open to a relatively easy attack from a hacker. To reduce the risk, make sure that you install a firewall device that prevents access from external users. Here are the basic security measures that you should implement:

▨ Install network access control software or hardware – usually a firewall. This checks any user as they try and access your network and will stop any unauthorised users – such as hackers – gaining access or viewing your local files. If you are installing a router, used to provide shared Internet access, many provide basic firewall features and prevent other Internet users and hackers gaining access to your network.

▨ If you have just signed up to the ADSL standard for high-speed links to the Net, you are also entering a higher-risk category. The problem with ADSL is that it is *always on* – your computer or network is always connected to the Internet, making it an easier target for hackers. If you connect through ADSL you must fit a firewall or similar access control device.

virus attacks

Just about any file you download could contain a virus, but in reality the number of incidents is very low. However, if your PC or your company's network gets infected, it can be very damaging – so protect your computers now. Viruses are tiny, highly sophisticated programs that take advantage of a loophole in a computer system or software application. They normally burrow into another *carrier* file – often a computer program or sometimes an e-mail message, or a Word or Excel document (these macros in documents are called macro viruses). Many viruses are benign, but some can delete or corrupt your computer files.

When you open or run the carrier file, the virus wakes up and does two things: first, it tries to spread to other similar files – to *infect* them; next, it might try and wreak havoc on your computer. Many viruses are harmless, but annoying, and simply spread themselves, but the majority will try and delete files, crash your hard disk or corrupt information stored in files.

You cannot catch a virus simply by downloading a file. However, if the file you download is infected with a virus, you will catch it when you open or run the file. If you download a file or receive a file through an e-mail attachment, it could also contain a virus, so you have to be particularly careful when dealing with attachments received from an unknown e-mail address.

Only a few types of file do not contain viruses: notably image files and simple Web pages (however, many Web pages use extra programs, called applets, to provide multimedia or special effects – and these could contain a virus).

To stop any potential problems, never open e-mail attachments from users you do not know. Always scan newly downloaded files with a special software program that can detect and remove viruses – before you open the file. Lastly, install background scanning software on the company server to ensure that the main files are protected. Two of the most popular virus detection programs are McAfee (www.mcafee.com) and Norton AntiVirus (www.symantec.com).

getting online – directory

e-mail software

▨ Outlook Express	www.microsoft.com
▨ Eudora	www.qualcomm.com
▨ Pegasus	www.pegasus.usa.net

free e-mail accounts

▨ Bigfoot	www.bigfoot.com
▨ Cometmail	www.cometmail.com
▨ Excite!	www.excite.com
▨ Hotmail	www.hotmail.com
▨ RocketMail	www.rocketmail.com
▨ Yahoo!	www.yahoo.com

finding an e-mail address

▨ AltaVista	www.altavista.com
▨ BigFoot	www.bigfoot.com
▨ Excite	www.excite.com
▨ Four11	www.four11.com
▨ Who Where	www.whowhere.com

newsgroup readers

Agent   www.forteinc.com
Gravity   www.microplanet.com
Hogwasher   www.asar.com
Messenger   www.netscape.com
News Rover   www.newsrover.com
NewsWatcher   www.filepile.com
News Xpress   www.download.com
Outlook Express   www.microsoft.com

finding and searching newsgroups

Deja   www.deja.com ·
Newsgroup Directory   www.tile.net
Usenet Info Center   http://metalab.unc.edu/usenet-i/

management and filter software

CyberPatrol   www.cyberpatrol.com
Cybersitter   www.cybersitter.com
GFI Communications Ltd.   www.gficomms.com
NetNanny   www.netnanny.com
NHA   www.nha.com
Omniquad   www.omniquad.com
SurfWatch   www.surfwatch.com

anti-virus software

McAfee   www.mcafee.com
Net Paradox   www.netparadox.com
NHA   www.nha.com
Norton AntiVirus   www.symantec.com
Omniquad   www.omniquad.com

glossary

access log   record of every visitor to your website, together with details of when they visited and which pages they viewed. This log file is created automatically (just ask your ISP or hosting company to switch on the feature); use the results to see who visits when, which pages are most popular – if you set up special pages for ad-response, it is easy to check the success of the campaign.

access provider   see *ISP*.

address (e-mail)   the unique name that identifies a particular person or account (a temporary store) for messages. For example, a unique personal e-mail address would be *simon@workingsite.com*

address (website)   the unique set of words (or numbers) that identify the location of a website on the World Wide Web (www). Sometimes called a URL (uniform resource locator). For example, *www.workingsite.com* and *www.Microsoft.com* are two unique website addresses.

address book   feature of an e-mail program that lets you store a list of contacts with their e-mail addresses.

ADSL   asymmetric digital subscriber line. The latest high-speed system of connecting to the Internet – several times faster than ISDN – but at a fixed, flat monthly subscription that has no per-minute call charges. In the UK, British Telecom's ADSL scheme is called OpenWorld (*www.bt.com/openworld*) and other ISPs are starting to offer the service at around £40 per month.

antivirus program   special software that will check all the files on your hard disk to detect and remove viruses from program and document files. Always use antivirus software to check any new file you download from the Internet or receive as an attachment through e-mail.

applet   a small program that is downloaded from a website and runs within your Web browser. Often used to provide special multimedia effects or for some shopping-cart systems.

attachment   one or more files (such as a document or spreadsheet) sent within an e-mail message.

authentication   a system that allows a company to prove that it is what it claims to be; the system is used to set up secure websites (see *SSL*) and uses a unique electronic certificate issued by independent certifiers to the company. The independent certifiers include VeriSign (*www. verisign.com*) and Thawte (*www.thawe.com*).

banner ad   the low, wide oblong-shaped advertising panels that appear on just about every commercial website. Banner ads advertise a product or service or website and entice users to click on them and jump to the advertiser's website. See also *click through* and *impression*.

bookmark   a feature of Web browser software that lets you store the address and description of a website in an address book within the browser. When you want to revisit the site, just select the bookmark entry. Microsoft calls this feature *Favorites*.

bounce   an e-mail message that could not be delivered and so has been returned to the sender. Sometimes this is because of a problem with the connection or the server, but is usually because the e-mail address is wrong.

bps   bits per second. See *bit*.

certificate   a unique set of numbers issued to a company as proof that it is what it claims to be; used by companies when implementing a secure website (see *SSL*); the certificate is generated by an independent trusted organisation (the two biggest are VeriSign and Thawte), once the company has satisfied the certifier that it is legitimate. The company needs this certificate to install a secure website feature, normally used on a shopping or commerce site.

CGI   common gateway interface. System that lets a Web page send information to a program running on the server; used with specialist programs written to add features to a website. For example, if you want to add a search feature or discussion group, the program that carries out the function transfer information to the Web page uses CGI. The programs are normally written in the *Perl* language.

click through   measure of the number of viewers that click on a banner advert (and so jump to the advertiser's website). Used as a way of charging the advertiser for the advert. A click through rate of just a few per cent is common; most advertisers have to pay per impression – a less attractive scheme than paying per click through (where you effectively pay for results).

cookie   a tiny file stored on your computer by a website. The file can contain information such as your user name at the site, when you last visited, or the last item you purchased. Sometimes vilified, but normally harmless and usually required for a shopping site to work at all.

CPA   cost per action. The cost of one impression (the action of displaying) a banner ad.

CTR   click through rate. The cost of one click through for a banner ad. It is not very common to see ad rates displayed in this format (where you pay for results); instead it is more usual to pay a CPA rate.

database   a collection of organised information that can be stored, searched and displayed – for example, your company's range of products, the office telephone directory, or an encyclopaedia. Adding a database to your website can be a big draw for visitors – if the content is worth searching for! However, it can be complex to add a database, although new software such as Microsoft FrontPage and FileMaker both provide relatively simple routes to publishing online. The traditional route is to use a custom-written program or, for vast complex systems (such as details of all the books available at a bookshop), a specialist commercial product, such as Oracle, is often used.

digital certificate   see *certificate*.

directory   a website that contains a list of links to other websites usually arranged in sections and often with a search feature. Yahoo! (*www.yahoo.com*) is one of the best-known directories and lists half a million websites. Search engines, such as Excite and AltaVista take a different approach and try and include every website on the net; directories are more selective.

domain name   a unique name that is used to identify one site (or server computer) on the Internet. For example, the domain name *microsoft.com* identifies Microsoft's main server that supports its website (with the address *www.microsoft.com*) and its e-mail system.

DNS (domain-name system)   a method of converting a domain name to the numerical IP (Internet protocol) address that is used to locate the computer within the Internet. The vast table of domain names and their IP addresses are stored on a domain-name server (also called DNS). For example, if you type in the domain name *www.microsoft.com* in your Web browser, this is passed to a DNS that translates the name to a set of numbers that points to the location of the Microsoft server computer.

download   to transfer information, usually a file, from a distant computer on to your own, usually through the Internet.

encryption   a system that can scramble text so that only the intended recipient can unscramble it and read it, protecting it against unauthorised viewing during its journey to the recipient.

FAQ   frequently asked question. List of, unsurprisingly, frequently asked questions and their answers. Most technical support sites provide a FAQ page to answer obvious and common questions.

firewall   a security system that protects a company's network of computers from access by hackers outside the company gaining access through the Internet. If you plan to link your company's network to the Internet, make sure that you also install a firewall to provide basic security measures against unwanted attention from outside the company.

folder   a container for your e-mail messages within an e-mail program or, on a hard disk, a container for files.

forward   to send on a message you have received to another user.

freeware   software that can be used on a permanent basis without charge. Compare with Shareware.

gateway   a link between two different types of system. For example, an e-mail-fax gateway provides/converts e-mail messages to the correct fax format, then resends it to a fax machine.

geotargeting   way of analysing and deducing where a website visitor is from or which location they are interested in, then displaying customised messages or advertisements; for example, if they ask for the weather in Seattle, you could display adverts from taxi companies in Seattle.

GIF   a graphics file format used to store images – one of two popular ways of storing graphics for a Web page. See also JPEG.

hit   technically, this is a request from a user's browser to view a particular page or image on your website. It is often misleadingly used as a measure of the popularity of a website or a measure of the number of visitors – it could, after careful processing, provide some of this information, but you will need to analyse your site's access log files to find these details. The problem occurs, because as each element within a Web page is displayed, it generates a *hit*. If your home page has three pictures and some text, every user will generate four hits in your access log. If they click on the refresh button on their browser, another four hits are recorded – just for one visitor.

home page   the initial page that is displayed when you visit a website. The home page is normally stored in a file called *index.html*. If you type in the website address *www.bbc.co.uk* you will automatically see the BBC home page on its website.

host provider see *Web space provider*.

HTML hypertext markup language. The codes and commands that are used to define and format a Web page. These commands let you define the colour, style and position of text, links and images within the page.

HTTP hypertext transfer protocol. The way in which a Web browser talks to a Web server to request information; it is actually a series of commands used by a browser to ask the Web server to transfer a particular page. Almost every full Web address (the URL) starts with these letters to tell the browser that you are typing in the address of a Web page, not an e-mail message or file transfer that both use related protocols.

hypertext a way of linking together Web pages over the Web. One word or section of text, or even an image on a Web page can be linked (this facility is often called a hyperlink) to jump to any other Web address on the site or on another site on the Web. When the user clicks on the link, they will see the referenced page displayed. It is the system that lets you browse the Web.

IE Internet Explorer. Microsoft's web-browser software.

impression the act of displaying a banner advertisement to a visitor on your website. If you want to pay for a banner ad to be displayed, you will probably be charged per impression – typical rates range from $50 to $200 per thousand impressions.

Internet or Net the millions of computers that are linked together around the world, allowing any computer to communicate with any other.

intranet a mini, private Internet that is only accessible to users on a company's internal network.

ISDN stands for integrated services digital network. A high-speed digital version of your standard old phone line. You will get a speedy connection to the Internet using an ISDN link, but you need a special modem (called a terminal adapter) and an ISP that provides ISDN access for its users. ISDN, however, is being overtaken by the new cable modem and ADSL technology.

Javascript programming language that lets web-page designers enhance the basic effects provided by HTML.

JPEG a graphics file format used to store images – often used to store photographic or high-quality images that can be displayed on a website.

keyword a word that you type in at a search engine to help you find relevant information.

link See *hypertext*.

Listserv See *mailing list*.

log analysis special software that converts the raw data recorded automatically each time a visitor looks at your website into graphs or tables that let you see clearly information such as how many visitors view the site and which pages are most popular.

logfile see *access log*

mailing list efficient, simple method of distributing information to a wide group of people who all share a common interest. The mailing list is simply a collection of e-mail addresses stored in a file; any message sent to the mailing list is automatically redistributed to all the users on the list. There are tens of thousands of mailing lists covering just about every possible subject area; to find something relevant, search *www.liszt.com*

mail server a computer on the Internet that manages and distributes e-mail messages ensuring that they are sent to the correct location.

meta-tags special information included at the top of the file that contains a Web page's HTML commands and used to help a search engine correctly index and summarise the contents of the page. By creating meta-tags, you are helping direct the search engine's indexing process to point towards the relevant or interesting features of your site.

modem a device that links your computer to a telephone line and allows you to dial into an ISP – and so connect to the Internet. A modem (*mo*dulator/*dem*odulator) converts your computer's data into sound signals that can be sent along a phone line.

newsgroup a public discussion forum where just about anything can be said. There are over 60 000 individual newsgroups on the Net (collectively called Usenet), each covering a particular subject or area of interest.

newsreader special software that lets you view and participate in a newsgroup; almost all current Web browsers include a newsreader feature.

offline not connected to the Internet.

online connected to the Internet.

opt-in mailing list   mailing list of e-mail addresses in which each person has agreed to receive advertising or marketing e-mail messages about a particular subject. If you rent an e-mail mailing list, make sure that it is an opt-in list.

page impression   a measure of how many times a Web page has been displayed to visitors. Often used as a crude way of counting the visitors to a site. See also *impression*.

page requests   a measure of the number of pages that visitors have viewed in a day. Often used as a crude way of indicating the popularity of your website. See also *log analysis*.

Perl   programming language that is particularly popular with developers creating custom applications for websites. Almost every commercial ISP (but usually the free ISPs) lets you write your own Perl programs to add a discussion group, shopping cart or chat session to your website.

PGP   pretty good privacy. Encryption system that is very secure and is a popular way of encrypting e-mail or a file so that only the intended recipient can decrypt and read the information.

post office   see *mail server*.

privacy statement   document included on your website that defines your company's policy regarding what it will (and hopefully will not) do with any personal information collected from visitors, such as their names and addresses submitted when ordering goods.

public domain   text, images or software that is freely available to anyone to view and use, but not resell. The copyright still remains with the original author.

secure site   a section of a website that implements a system (almost always the SSL system) to provide a secure channel between the website and your browser, ensuring that anything you type in (such as your credit-card details) cannot be read by a hacker.

server access logs   see *access log*.

shopping cart/basket   the electronic equivalent of a trolley that you would use in your supermarket. As you browse around an online shopping website, you can add products you want to buy to your shopping cart and when you have finished, pay for the goods by typing in your credit-card details.

signature   a unique authentication code (in a secure website) that identifies a company as part of its authentication certificate or the lines of text (in an e-mail) that are automatically added to the end of any e-mail you write (or newsgroup message that you post) and normally include your name, company name, slogan and basic contact details.

spam   an unwanted e-mail message sent in bulk to thousands of addresses to try and advertise something. Also refers to an advertising message posted to dozens of newsgroups at a time.

SSL   secure sockets layer. System that scrambles the data between your Web browser and the website in order to provide a secure channel. Used to create a secure section of a website where you can safely type in personal or credit-card details. Your browser indicates you are using a secure SSL page by displaying a tiny closed padlock icon in the bottom status bar of the windows.

unsolicited mail   advertising e-mail that you have not requested. Often called *spam*.

URL   uniform resource locator. The correct term for the full address of a Web page. For example, *bbc.co.uk* is a domain name, *www.bbc.co.uk* is the website address for the BBC and *www.bbc.co.uk/index.html* is the URL to the site's home page.

Usenet   see *newsgroup*.

Web browser   software that lets you view a Web page and navigate through the Web. New Web browser software (from Microsoft and Netscape) also includes an e-mail program and a news reader.

Web page   a single, discrete page within a website. Individual Web pages are stored in separate files that contain the HTML commands that describe layout of the page.

Web server   a computer that stores all the pages and images and other material that together forms a website (generally, Web servers store hundreds of separate websites or, in the case of mammoth sites from the BBC or CNN, several computers are used to store the website).

website   a collection of Web pages that together provide information about a particular product, person or company.

Web space provider   company that rents out Web space on its Web server computers where you can store the elements that form your website. Most ISPs provide you with Web space in return for your subscription.